Issue No. 12 — Emmett Magazine — December 2021

CONTENTS

Dori Jalazo

Artist/Writer Solos at The Artery in Greensboro, NC

Pages 4-8

Art By Emmett

Modern Madonna Christmas Card

Page 9

Top Ten

Book Publishers featuring EM 2020-2021

Page 10

Platinum Images Photography

Photographer: Anthony Lytle (Platinum Images Photography)
Web: https://www.platinumimagesphotography.com/
Photographer's IG: Platinum_Images
Model: Alexa
Model's IG: looksbyalexamarie
Makeup & hair stylist: Brittany Mims
Makeup & hair stylist IG: mimscreativeartistry
Modeling mentors: Yazzy Panamix & Mass Appeal DMV
Modeling mentors' IG: model.yazz & massappealdmv
Studio location: Ricke Brothers Auto Group
Pages 11-14 & Back Cover

Eleven55 Photos

ELEVEN55PHOTOS.COM

Photographer: Sowari Wilcox

Angie White Christmas Photo

Page 15

Issue No. 12   Emmett Magazine   December 2021

CONTENTS CONTINUED

Angie White Photos

Christmas & Cosplay

Models/Muses

Pages 16-29

Lady Cels Instagram IG @ladycels

Angie White/Pam White IG @mzpammb

Mrs. White/ Jackie/Nephew

Model Imari IG @imarialyce

Cheyenne IG @sheestheitgirl

Brianna IG @britheshknhealer

Emily Grace IG @egdramaqueen

Mike Becvar IG technicolormikeb

Geninne IG @womanofwonder8

Ponsella IG @ponsella_henry

Allison IG @mythril_arts

Brianna IG @brivivid

Stephanie IG @alston3128

Aaron Mills IG @undergroundartfactory

Angie White IG AWphotos84_

Virginia Kassay Q & A

with Emmett Williams

Pages 30-44

CONTRIBUTORS 2020-2021

Photographers

Angie White Photos

John Abbott Photo

Norman E. Jones

Candi Williams Photography

Platinum Images Photography

Eleven55 Photos

Sky Island Photos

Writers

Fred Little

Valerie Jones

Gabor

Virginia Kassay

SherylStyle

Models

Queen Kasha

Alexa

Radio/TV/Actress

DEE DEE WALKER

THE DEE DEE WALKER SHOW LIVE

(EMMETT WILLIAMS/ANGIE WHITE INTERVIEW)

Dori Jalazo

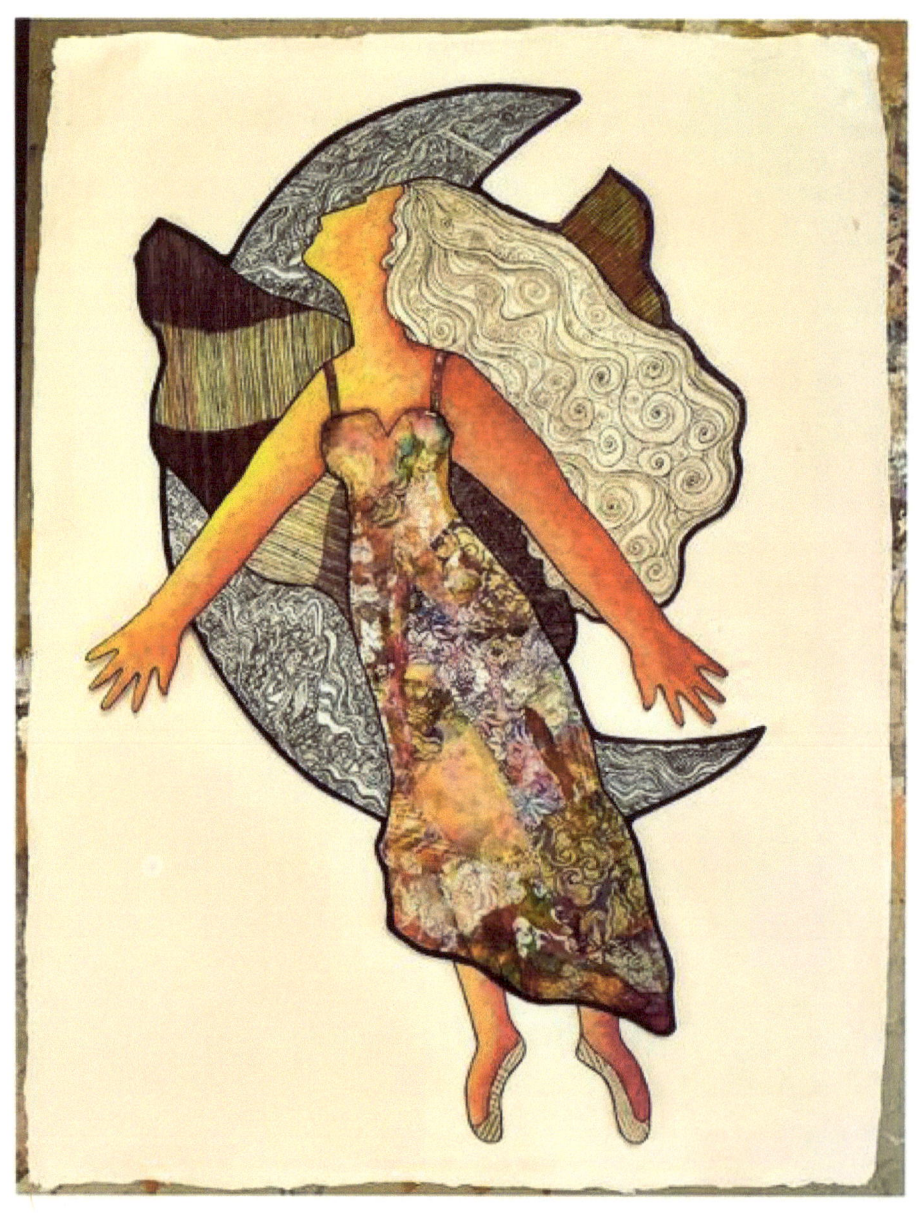

Issue No. 12 — Emmett Magazine — December 2021

Leap of Faith

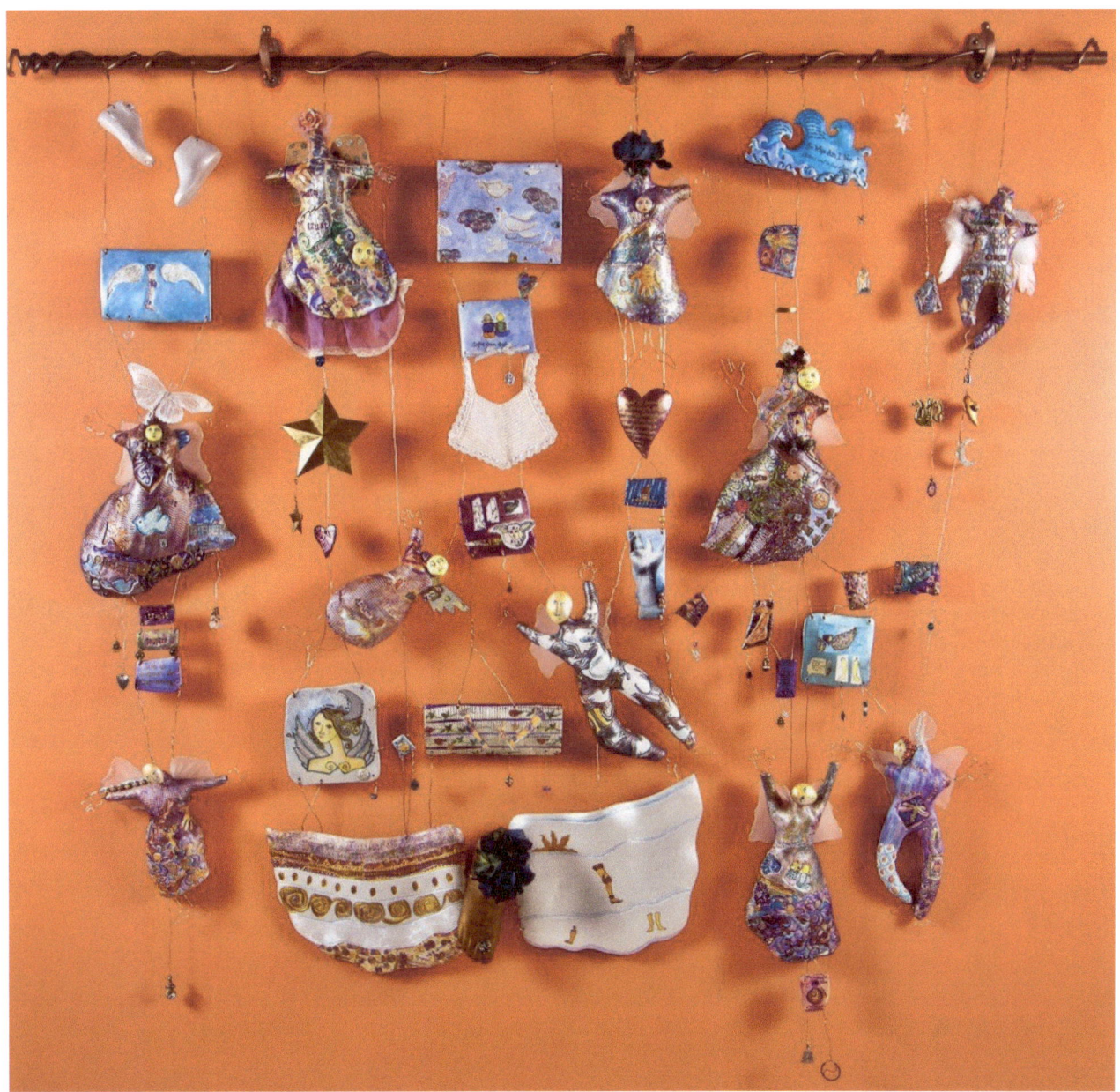

Ceramic Quilt

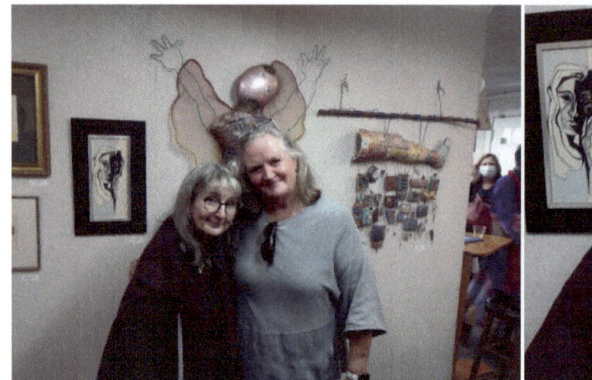
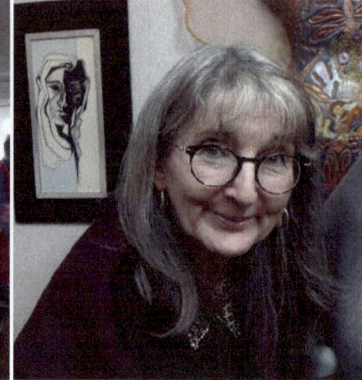
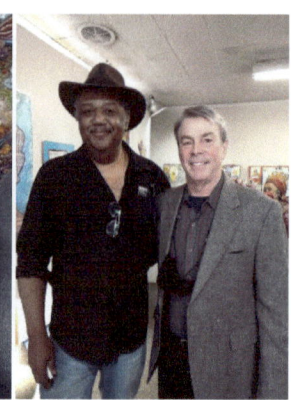

Dori Jalazo Solos at The Artery in Greensboro, NC

By Emmett Williams

Greensboro, NC, Dori Jalazo, Artist and Author of "One's Own Self" commanded a One Woman Show at The Artery in Greensboro, NC, located at 1711 Spring Garden Street. Numerous visitors arrived and wished well the Artist whose exhibition has been in the making for quite some time, during these difficult Covid-19 times we soldier through, in our cities.

Dori's time has finally arrived and her colorful empowering works are now on view.

The Artist chatted with me about a small pen and ink piece I focused on from her college years, which I found very compelling. She mentioned that it was created *in* her college years.

"I just adore pen & Ink!" The Artist stated.

Dori recently re-located an hour away from Greensboro, North Carolina.. She still puts in long hours perfecting her craft. The Artery's owner David, local Artist/Writer Jack Stone, PR/Arts Promoter Mebane Ham and others were in attendance for Jalazo's one-woman Show on Saturday December 4th, 2021.

"I was born in Newark, New Jersey. Then fate came in and both Paul and I moved to Allentown Pennsylvania when we were 9 years old and grew up together."

Paul would become a lawyer, and he and Dori married. "There are two areas of focus in my Art Life.

The new pieces painted with all kinds of media and collage pieces. I love looking deep into them. The colors, textures and symbols *move* me."

"The second area of Focus in my Art Life is the Art Installation. "Windows to My Soul"
The one you saw in Greensboro. I would donate it to the right collector or organization as long as they paid to have it shipped and fulfilled other criteria.

- My name should be connected to it in all ways.

- That it be available to be seen and experienced by those that need to know they are not alone, help them find their Voice, to speak their Truth.

- Hopefully it will travel so many can experience it."

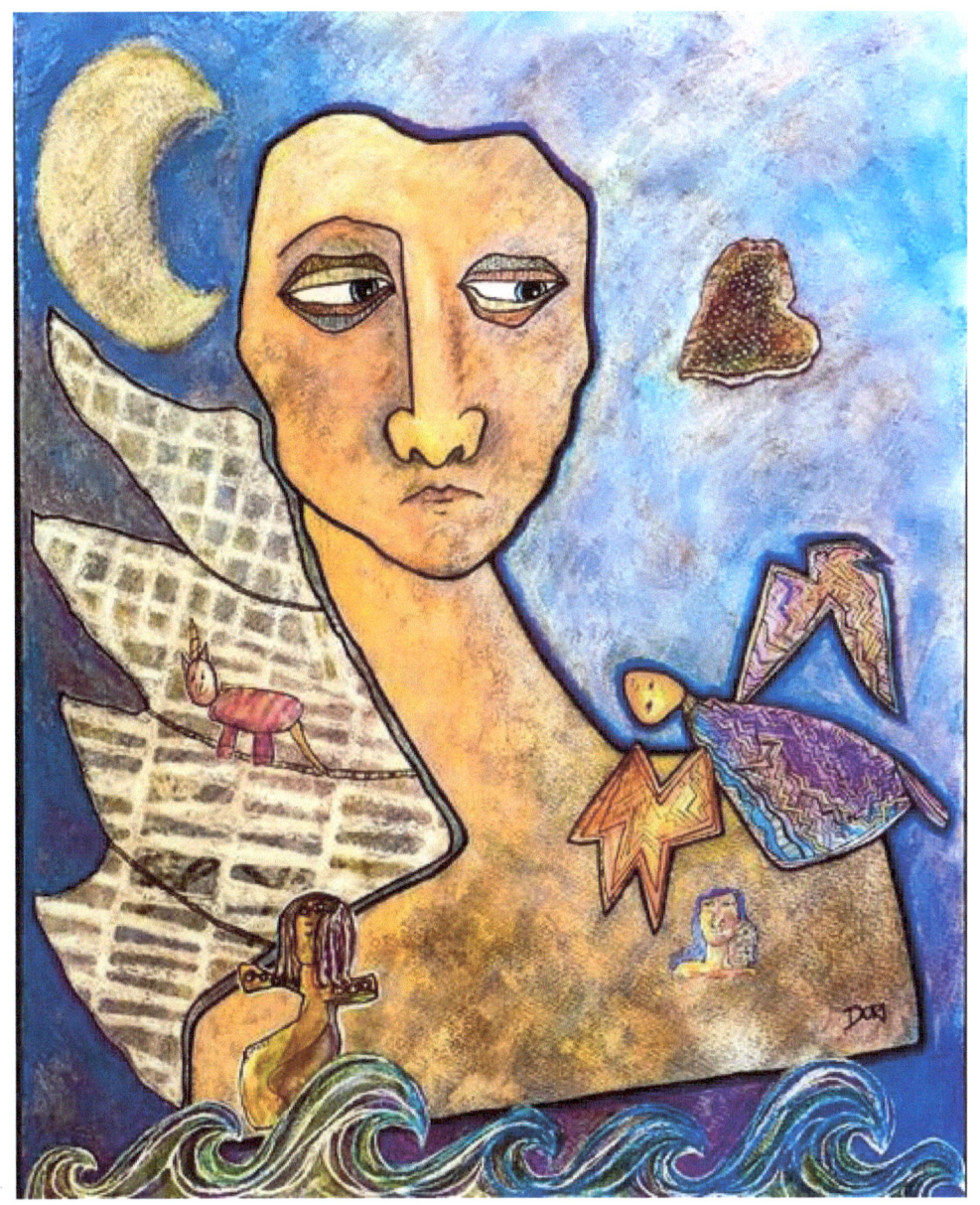

Angel on my Shoulders

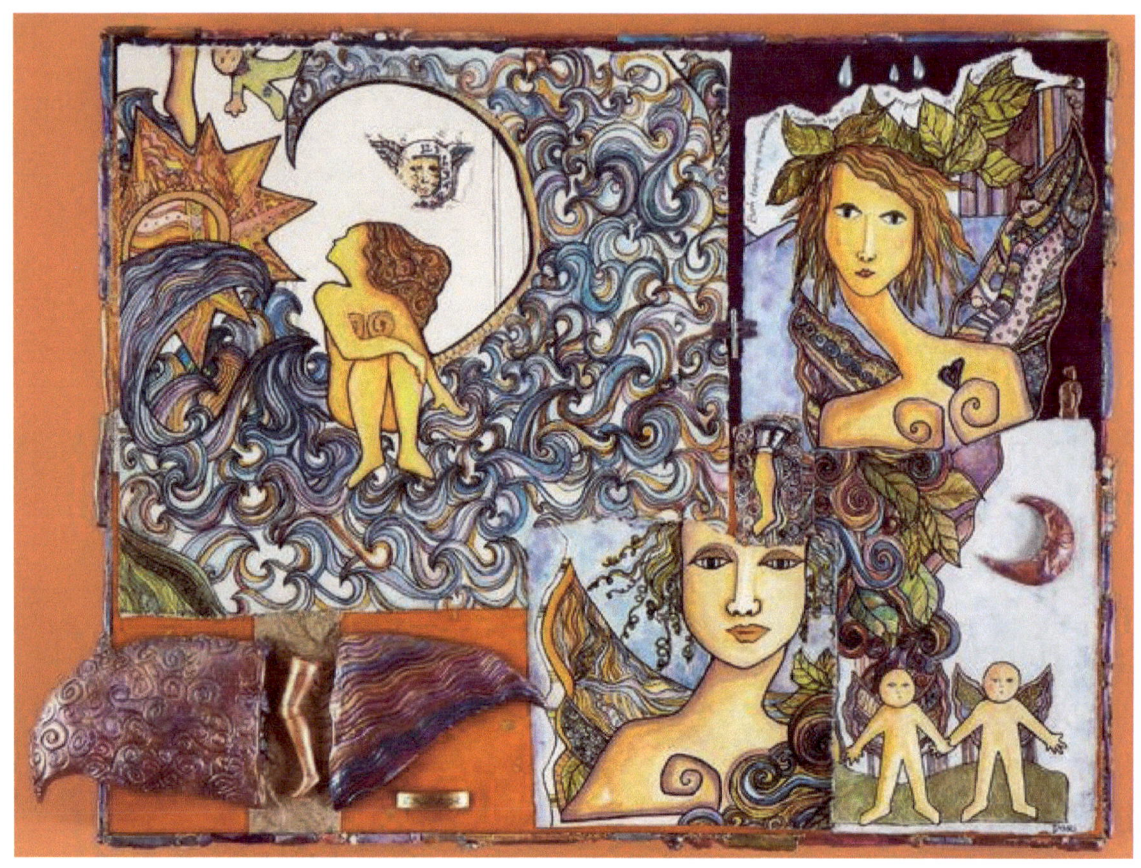

Both Rain & Teardrops

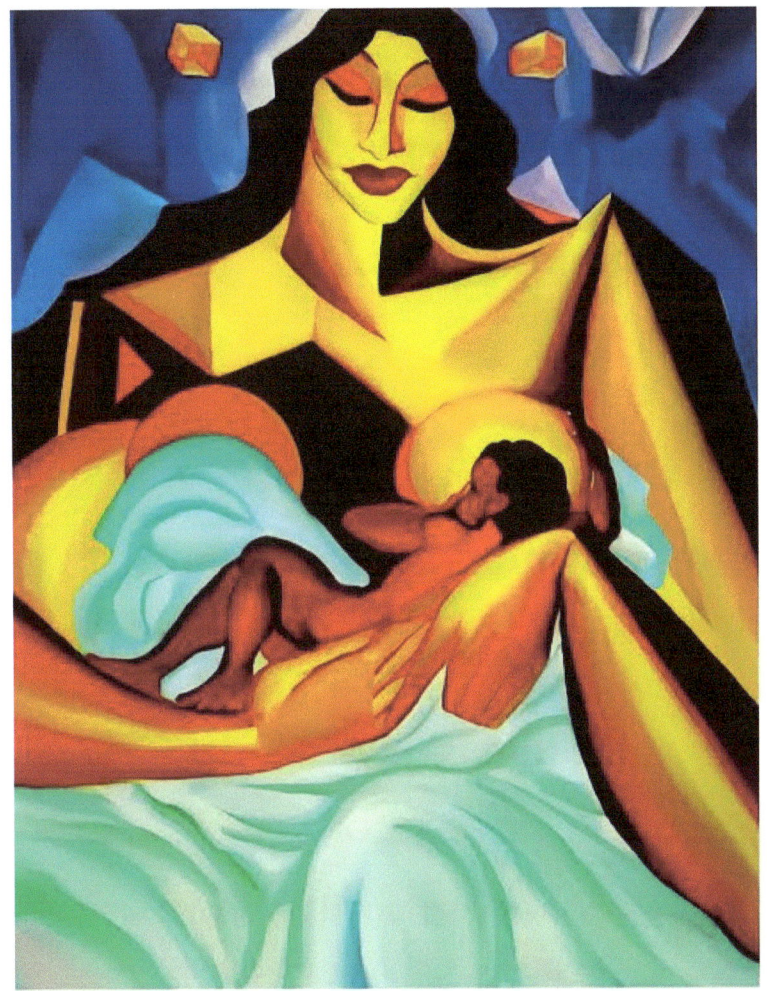

THE MODERN MADONNA BY EMMETT ARDIE WILLIAMS

Issue No. 12 Emmett Magazine December 2021

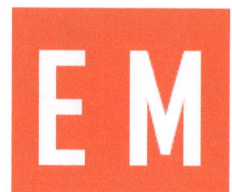

TOP 10

Amazon.com

AbeBooks.com

BetterWorldBooks.com

BooksAmillion.com

DiscoverBooks.com

Ebay.com

BarnesAndNobles.com

Blackwells.co.uk

Goodreads.com

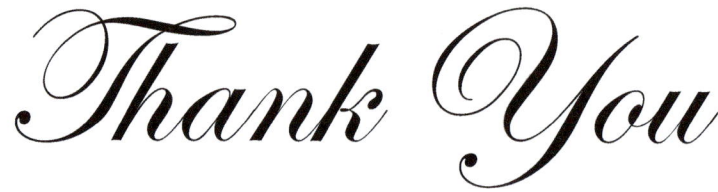

For featuring us on your websites 2020-2021

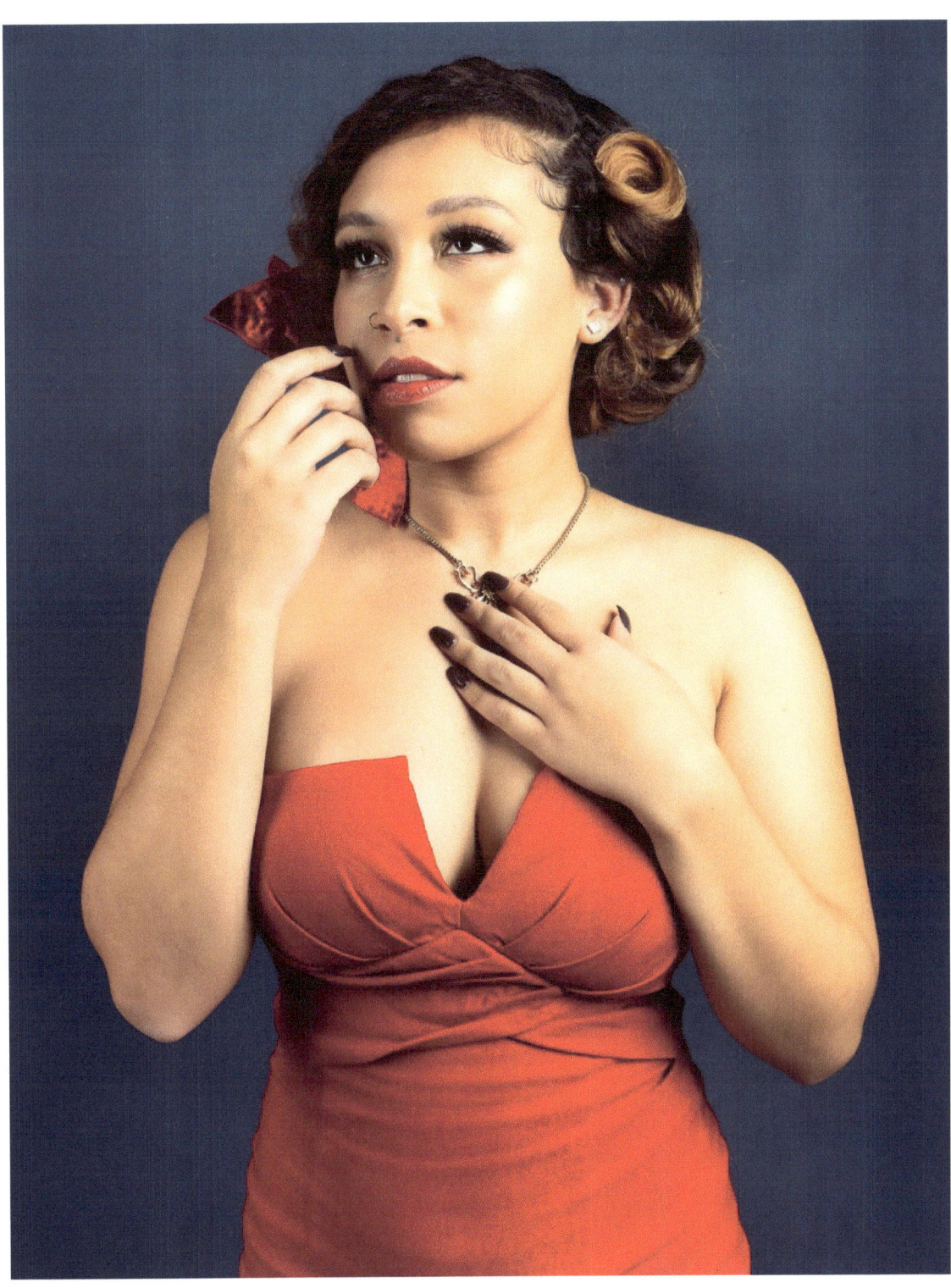

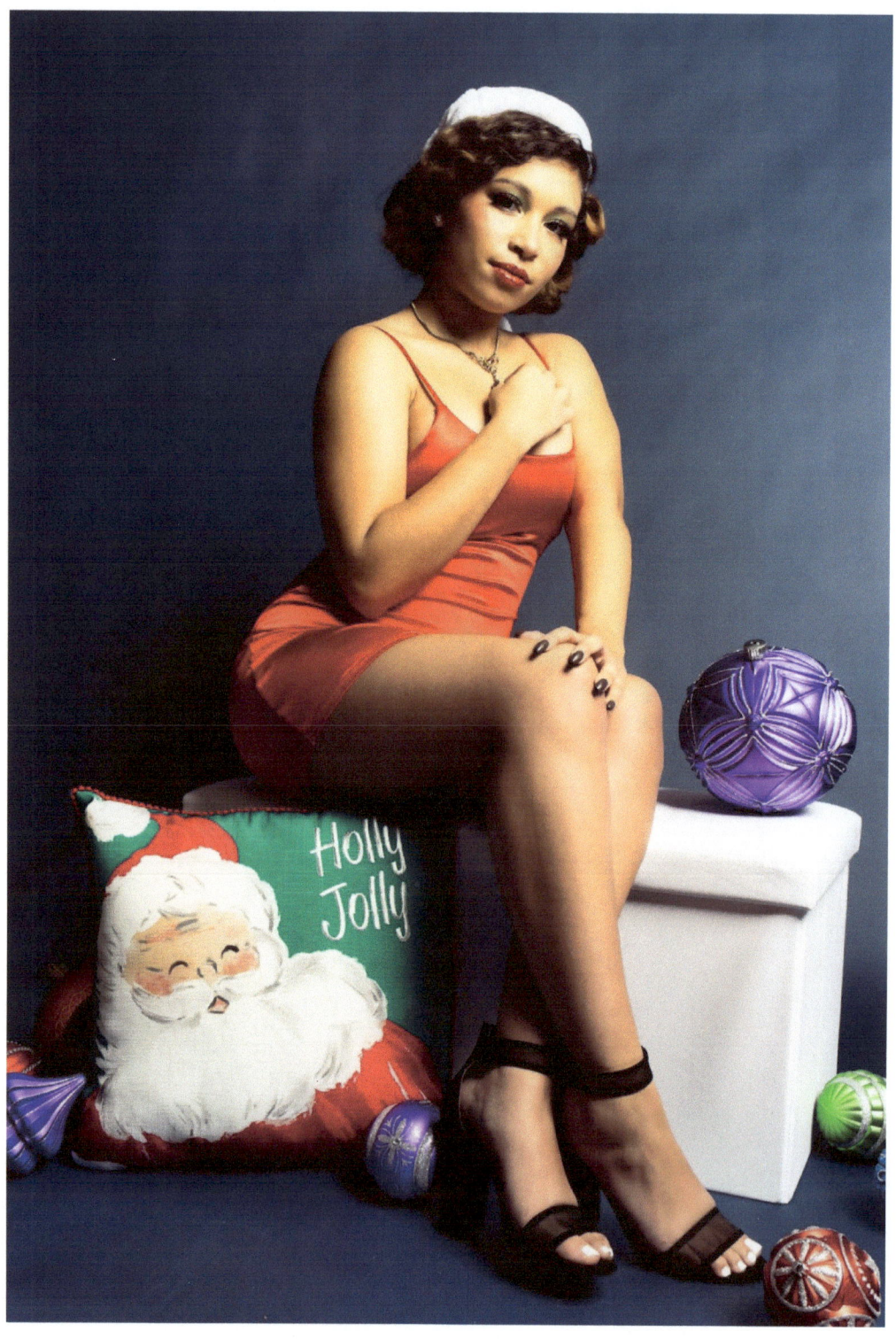

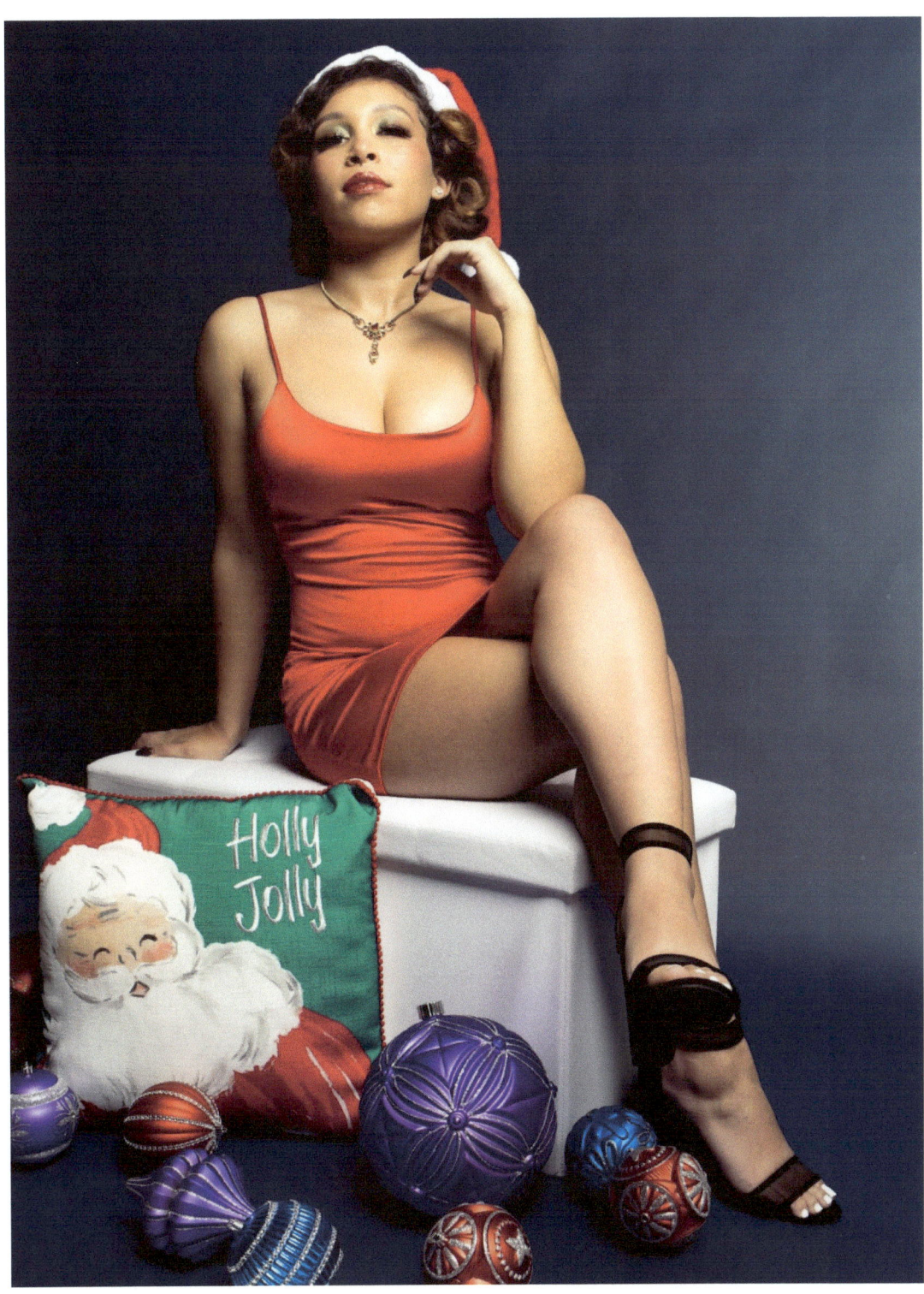

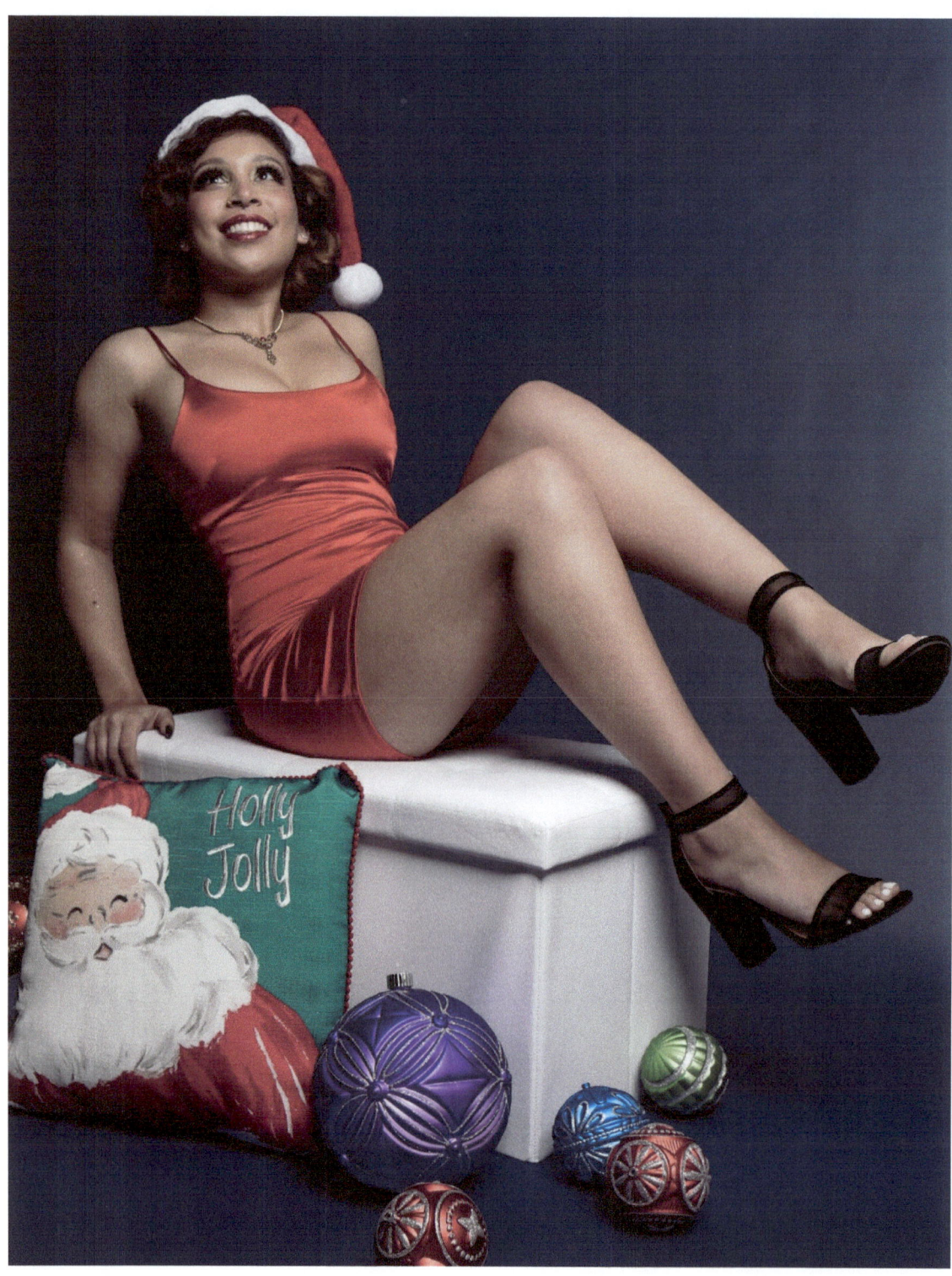

Issue No. 12 Emmett Magazine December 2021

Eleven55 Photos

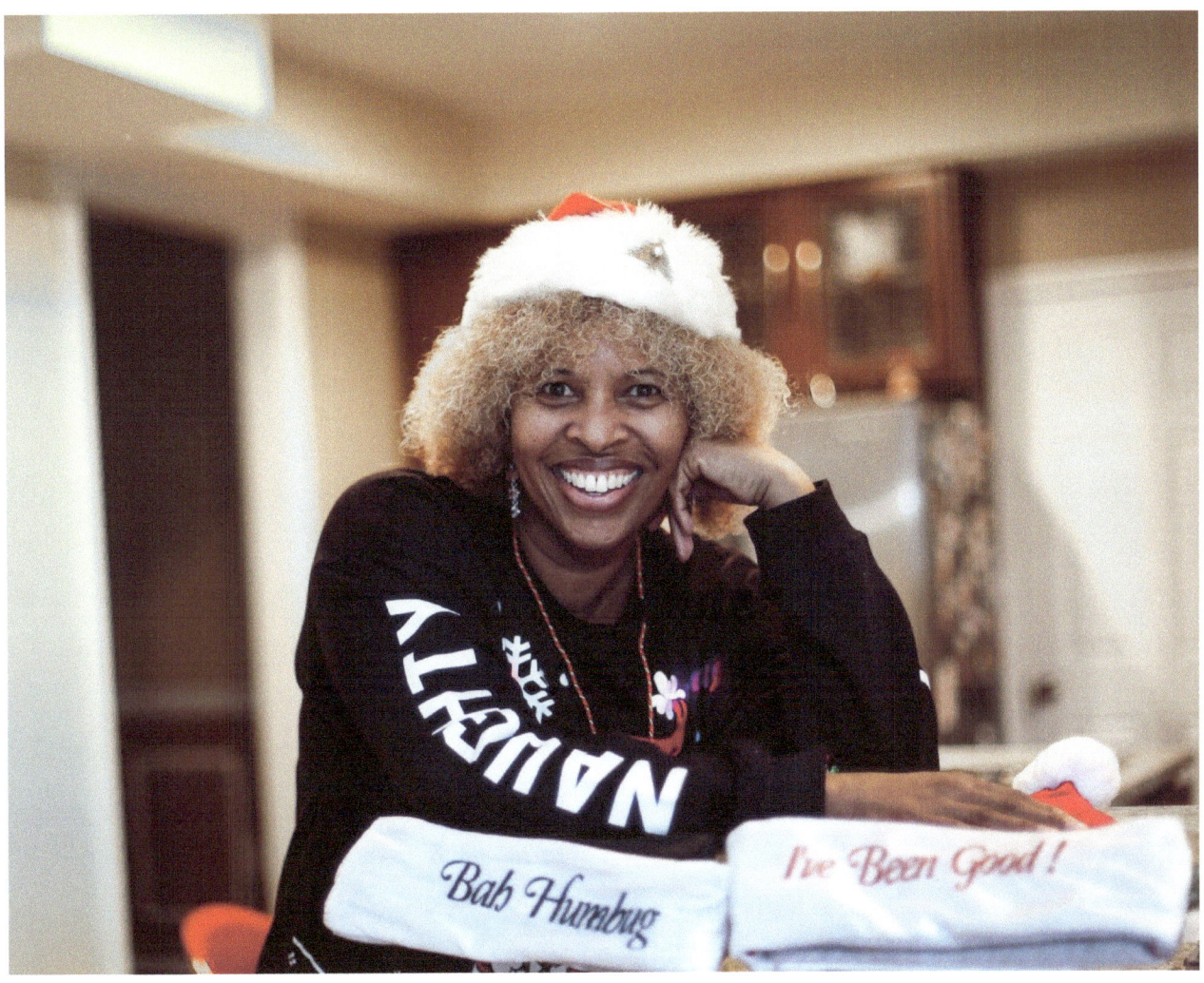

Thanks Angie for being a huge part of the magazine. When you need something done I always end up relying on soldiers. They know you need them to act on a moment's notice!

No better time than right now to go after and get your dreams fulfilled.

There will always be obstacles but creative people will figure it out and then help others do the same.

A friend recently said to me…"You're taking over the world!"

True…. Because it's doable!

-EM

Angie White

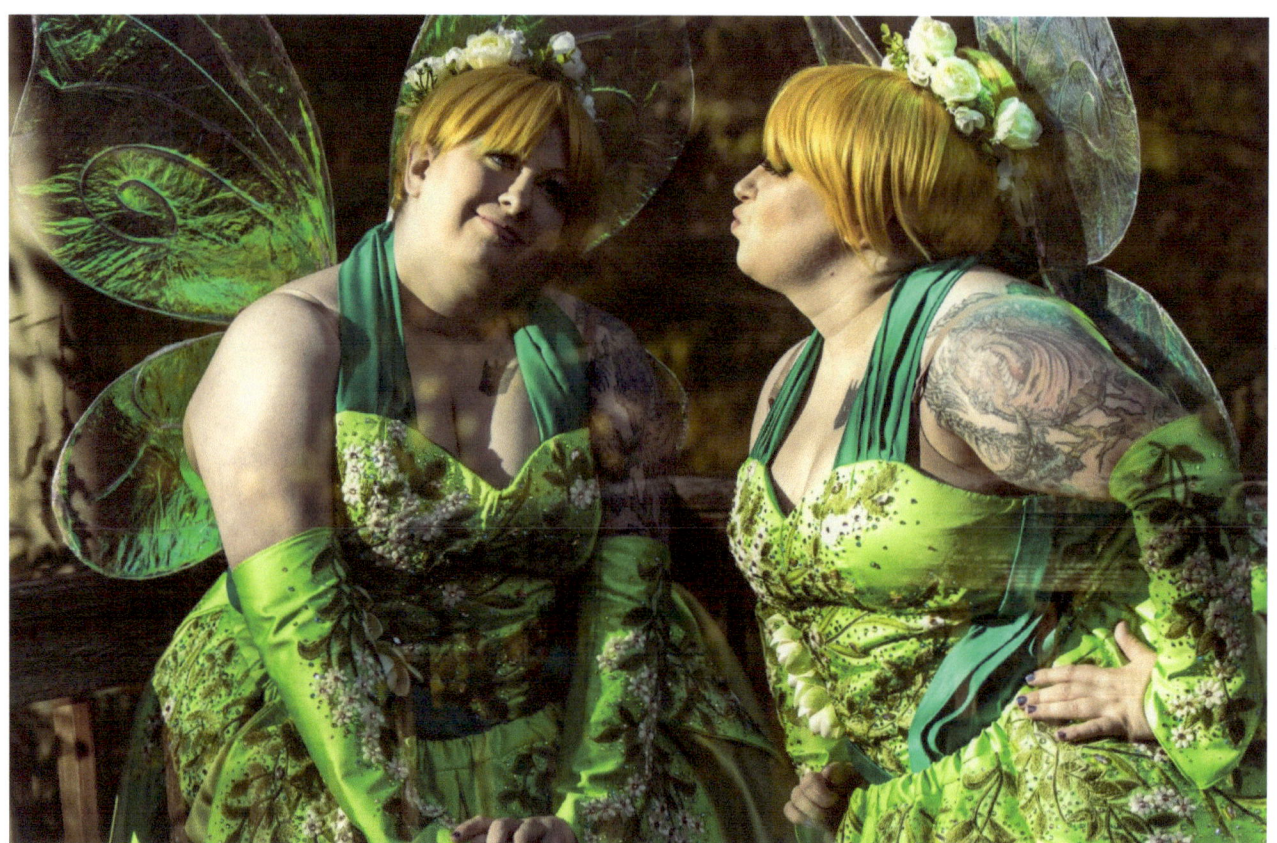

Christmas & Cosplay

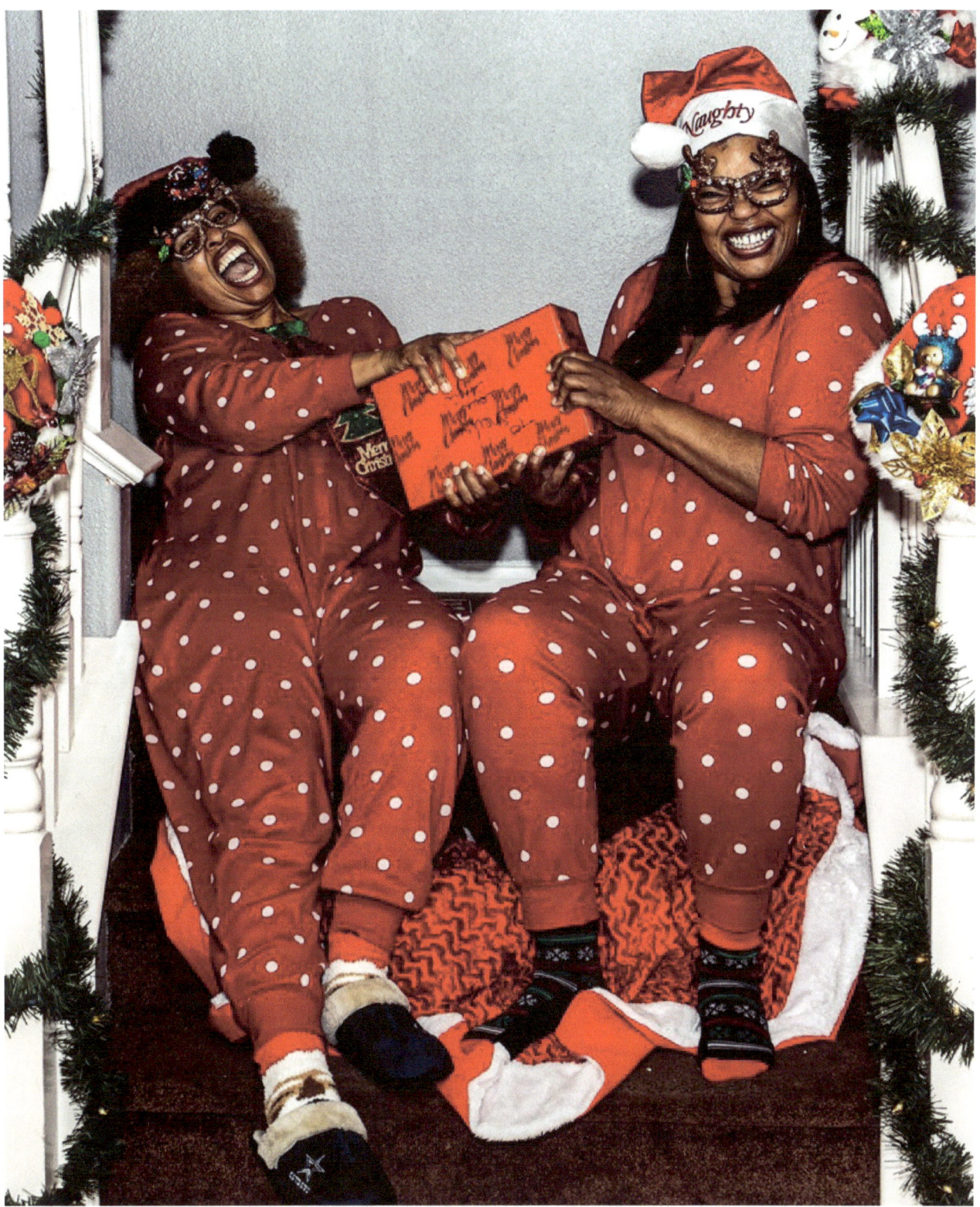

Issue No. 12 — Emmett Magazine — December 2021

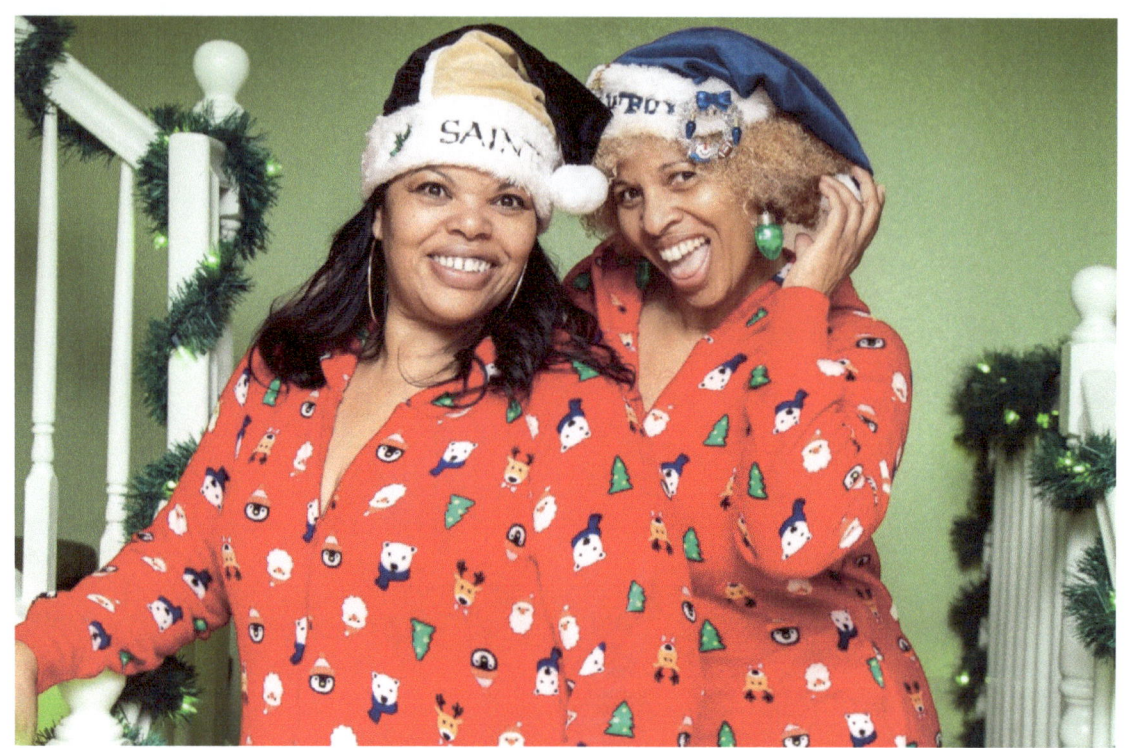

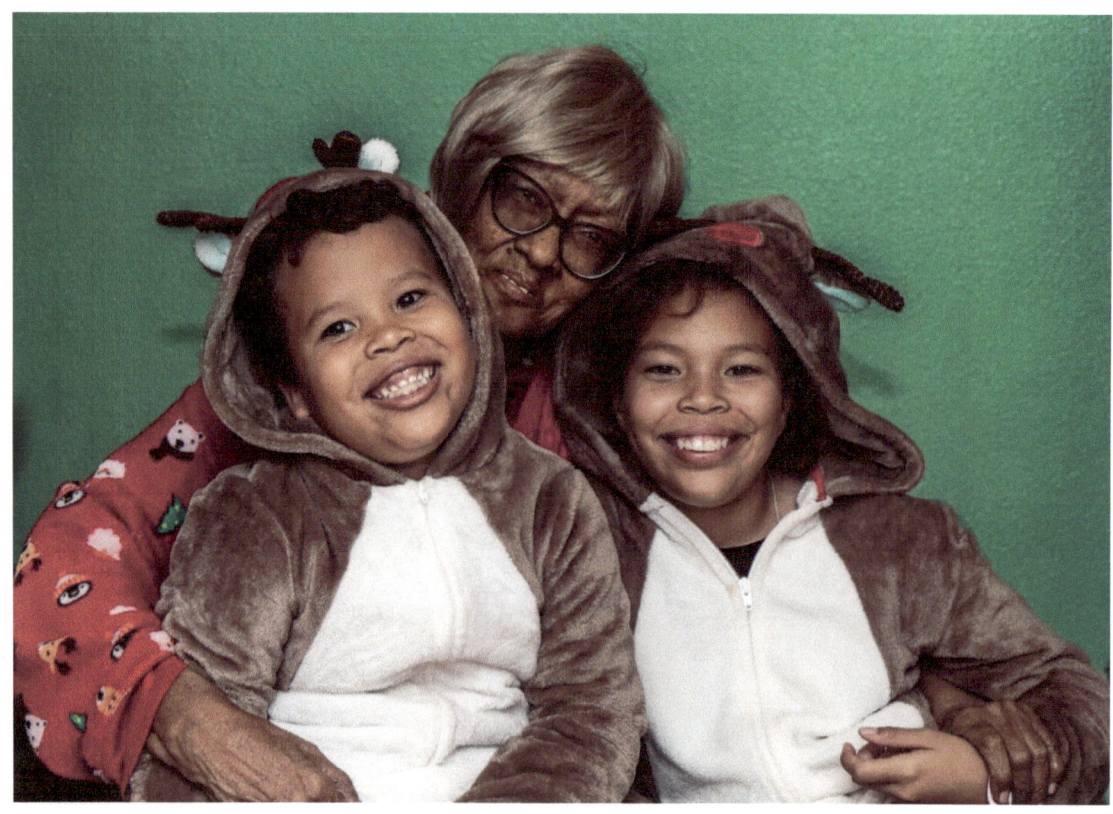

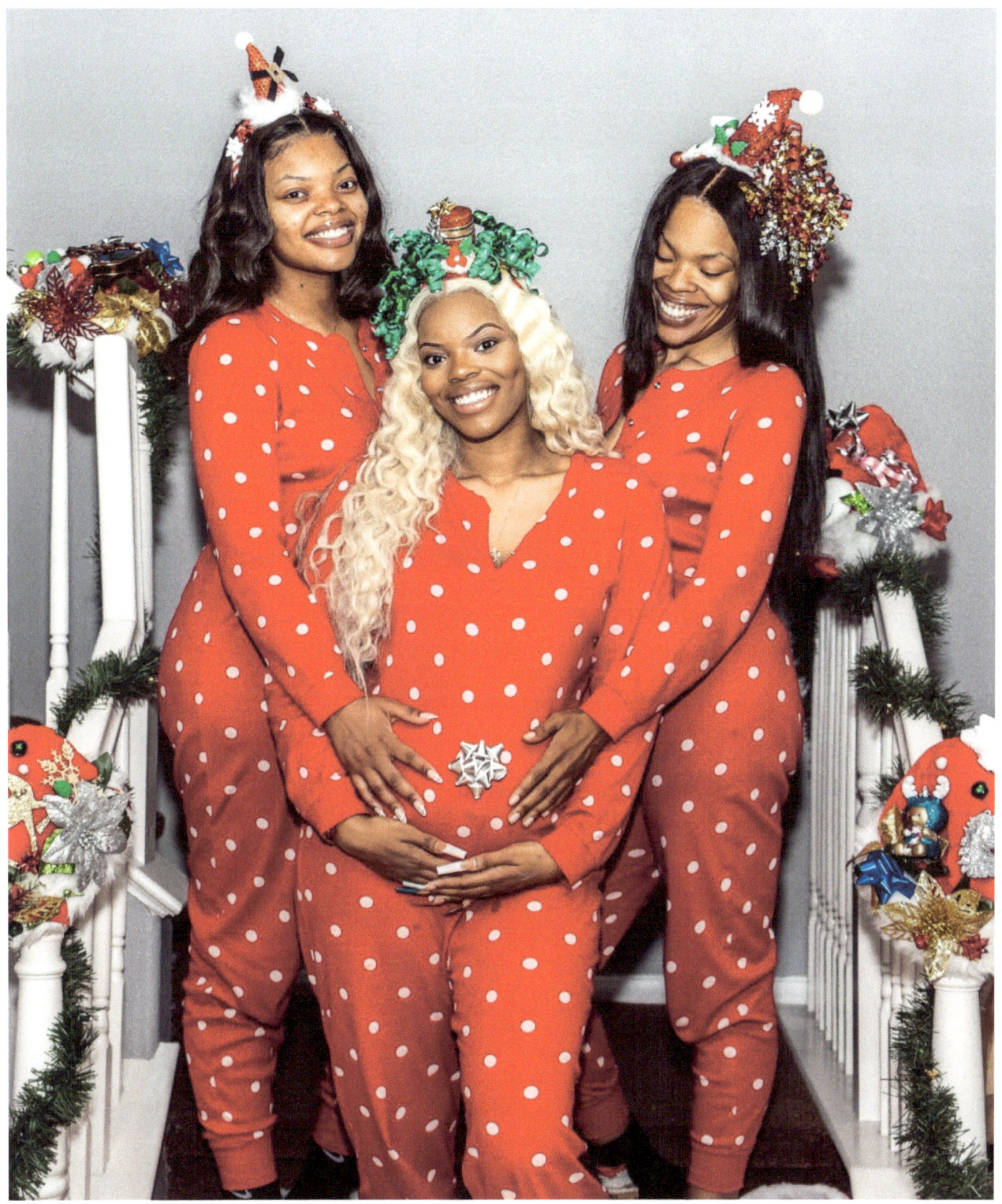

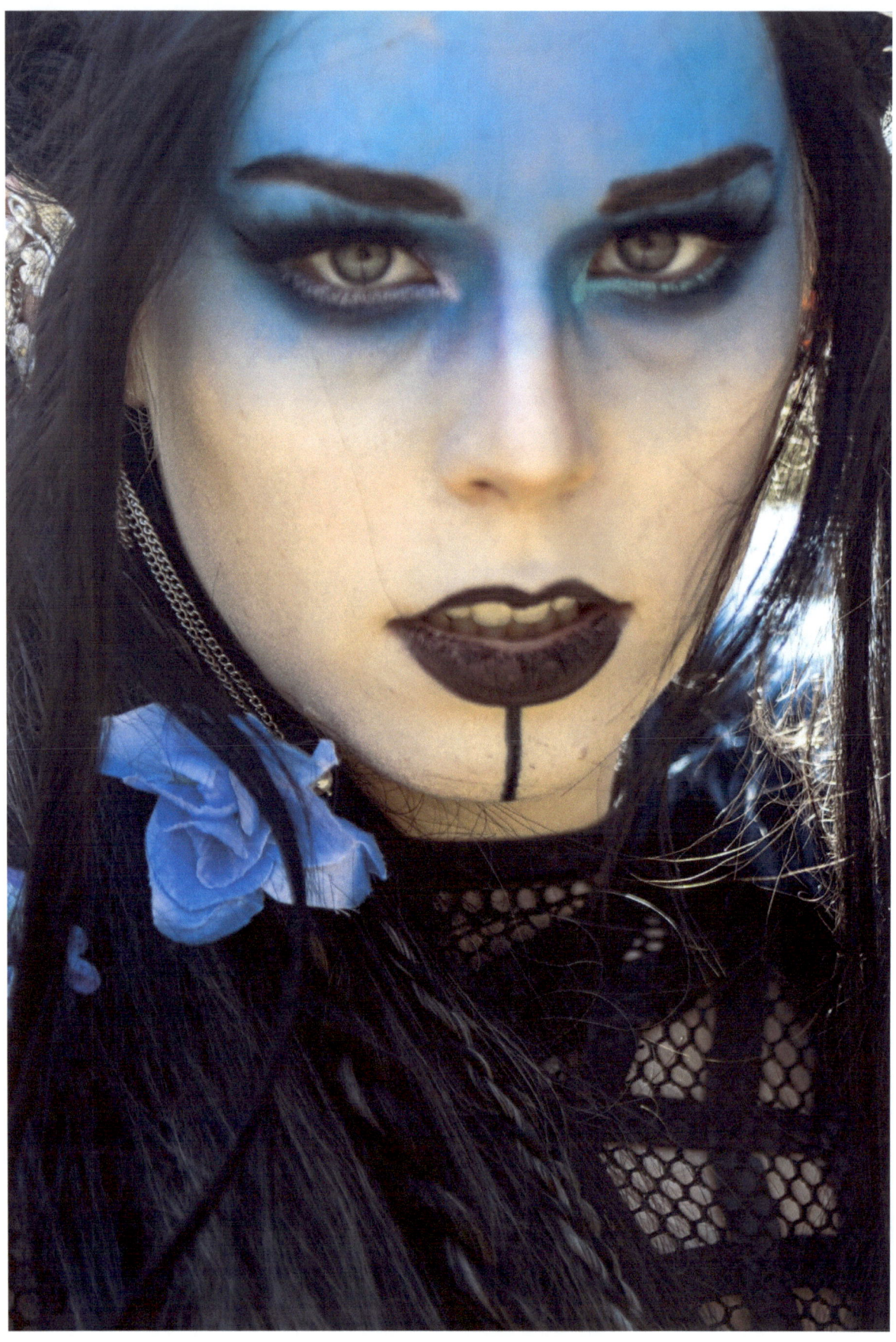

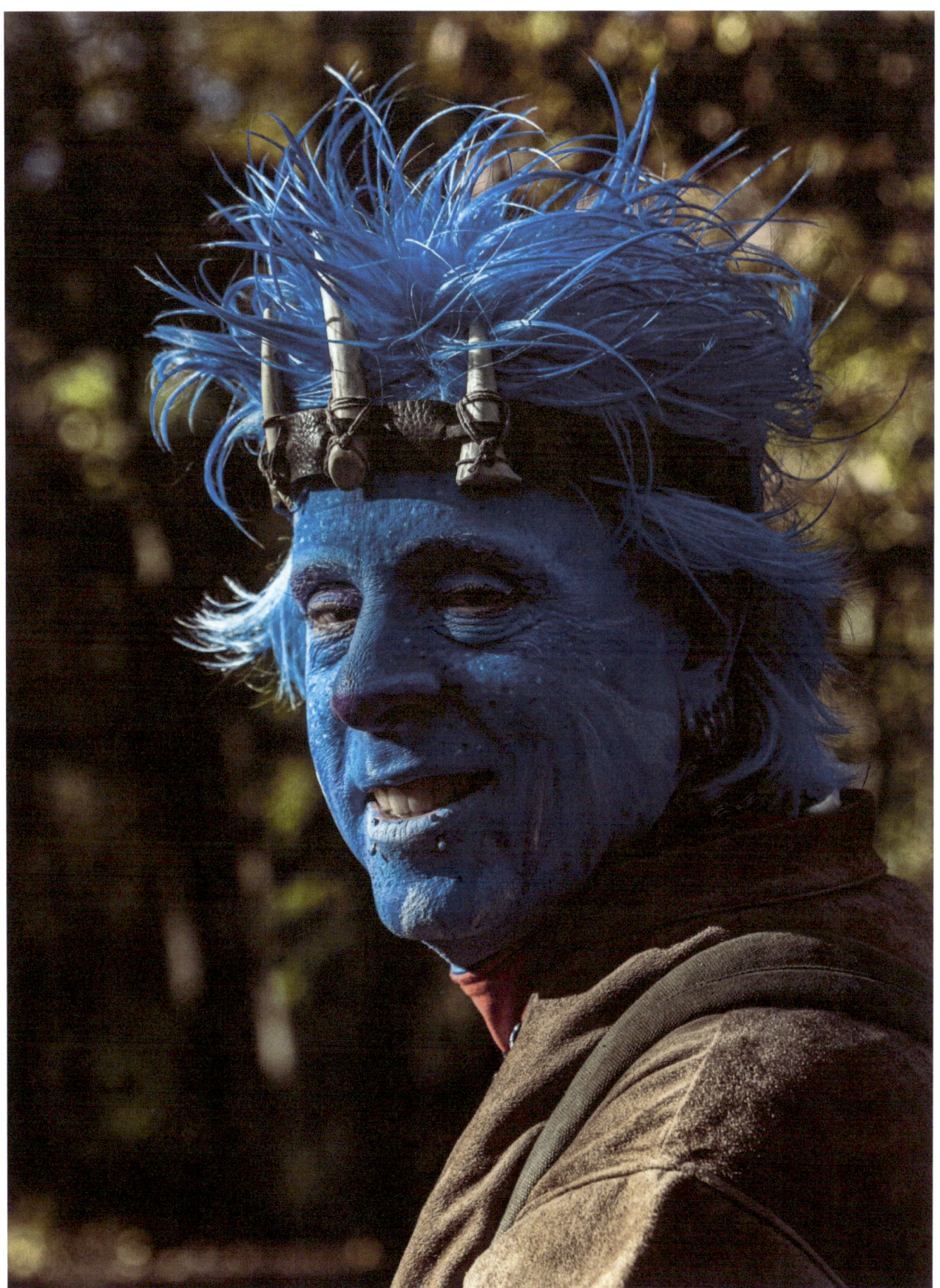

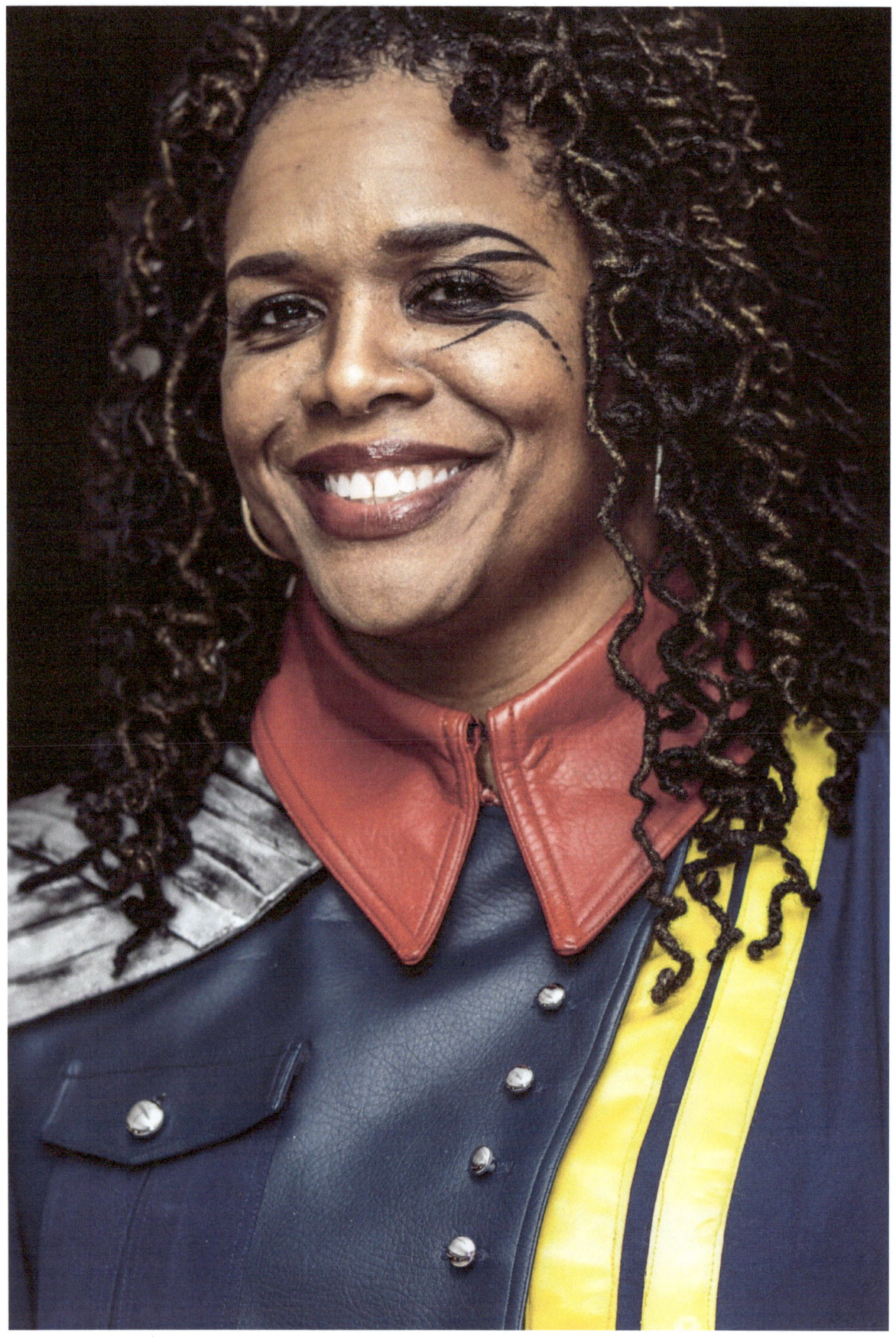

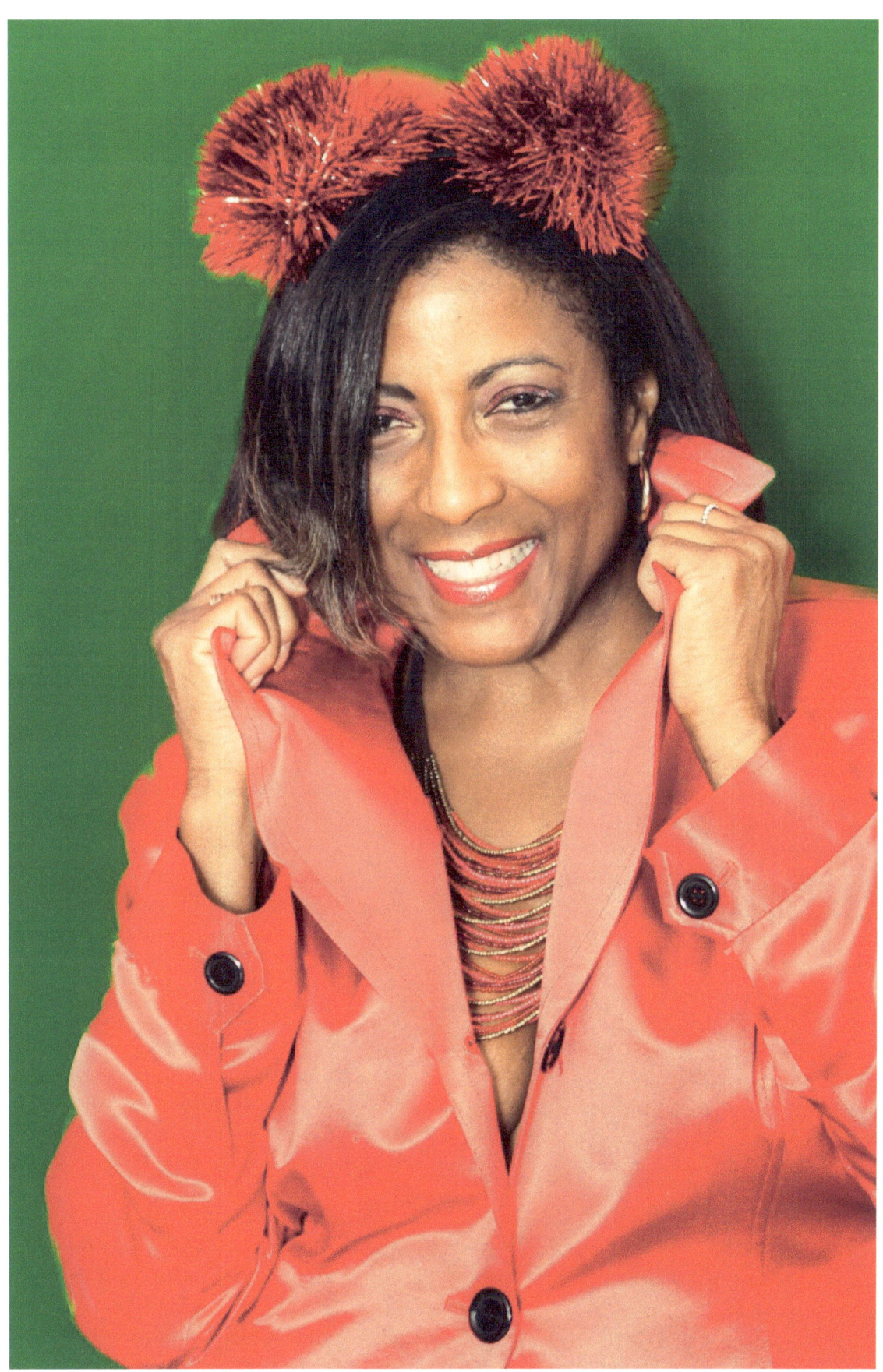

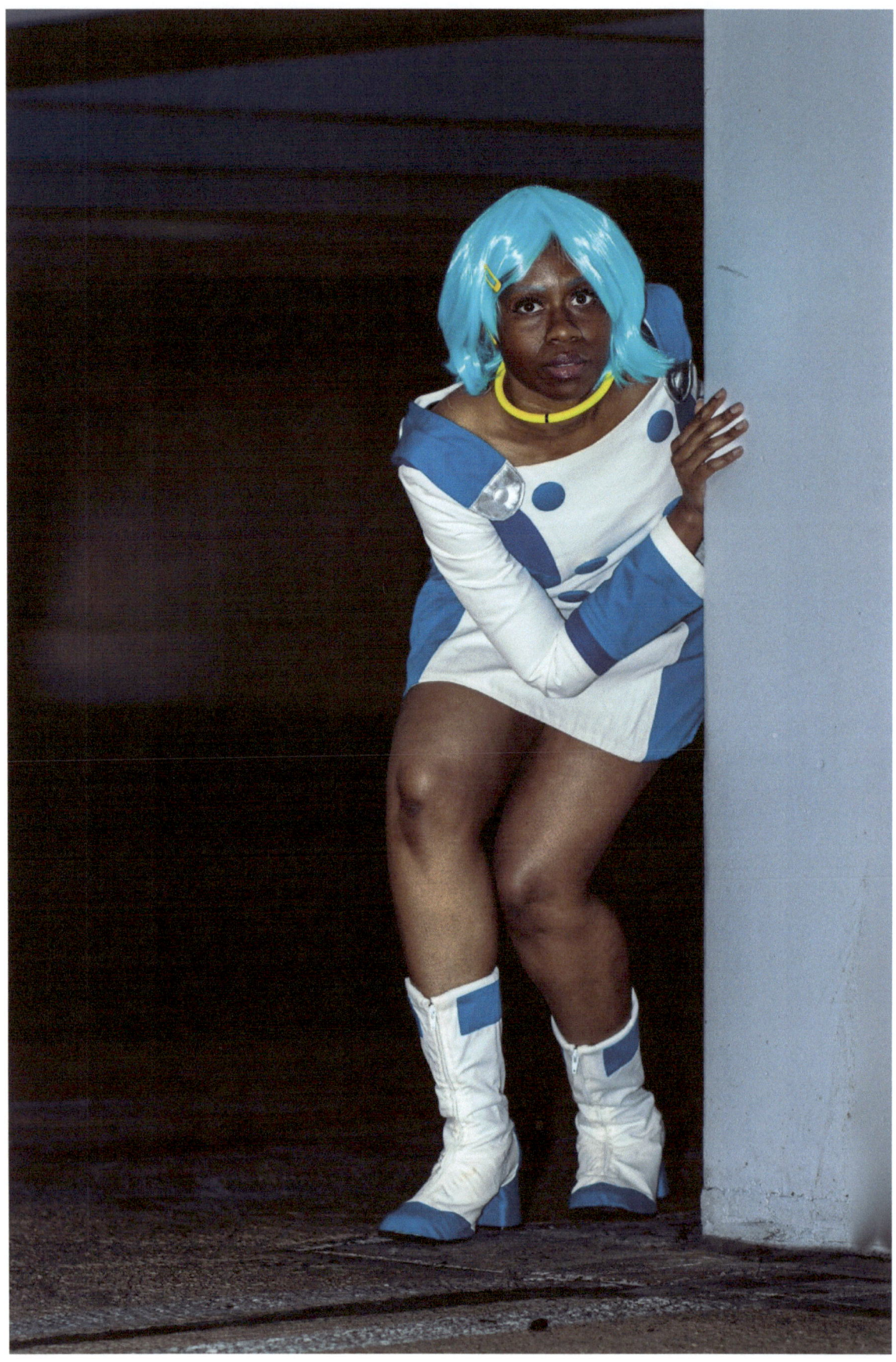

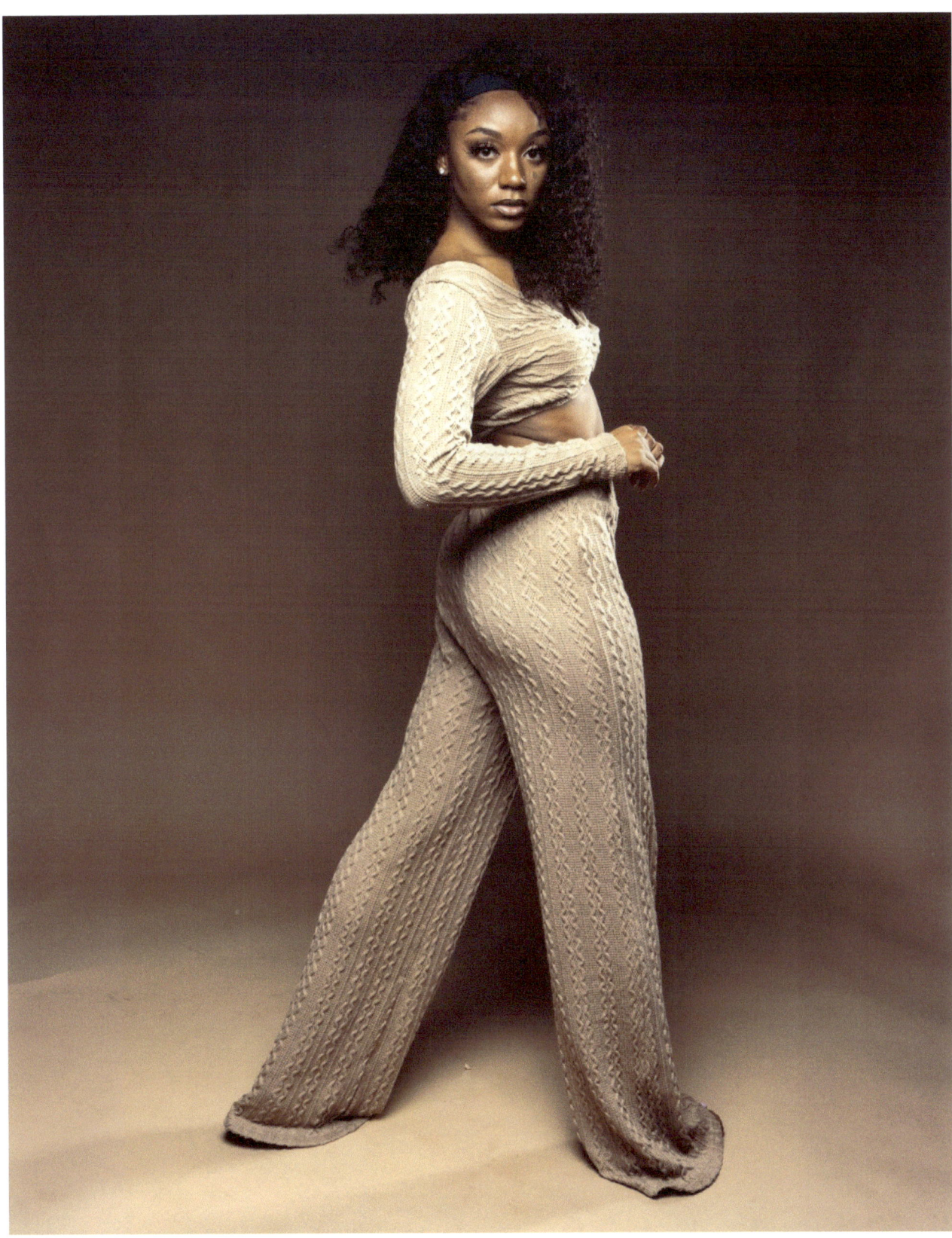

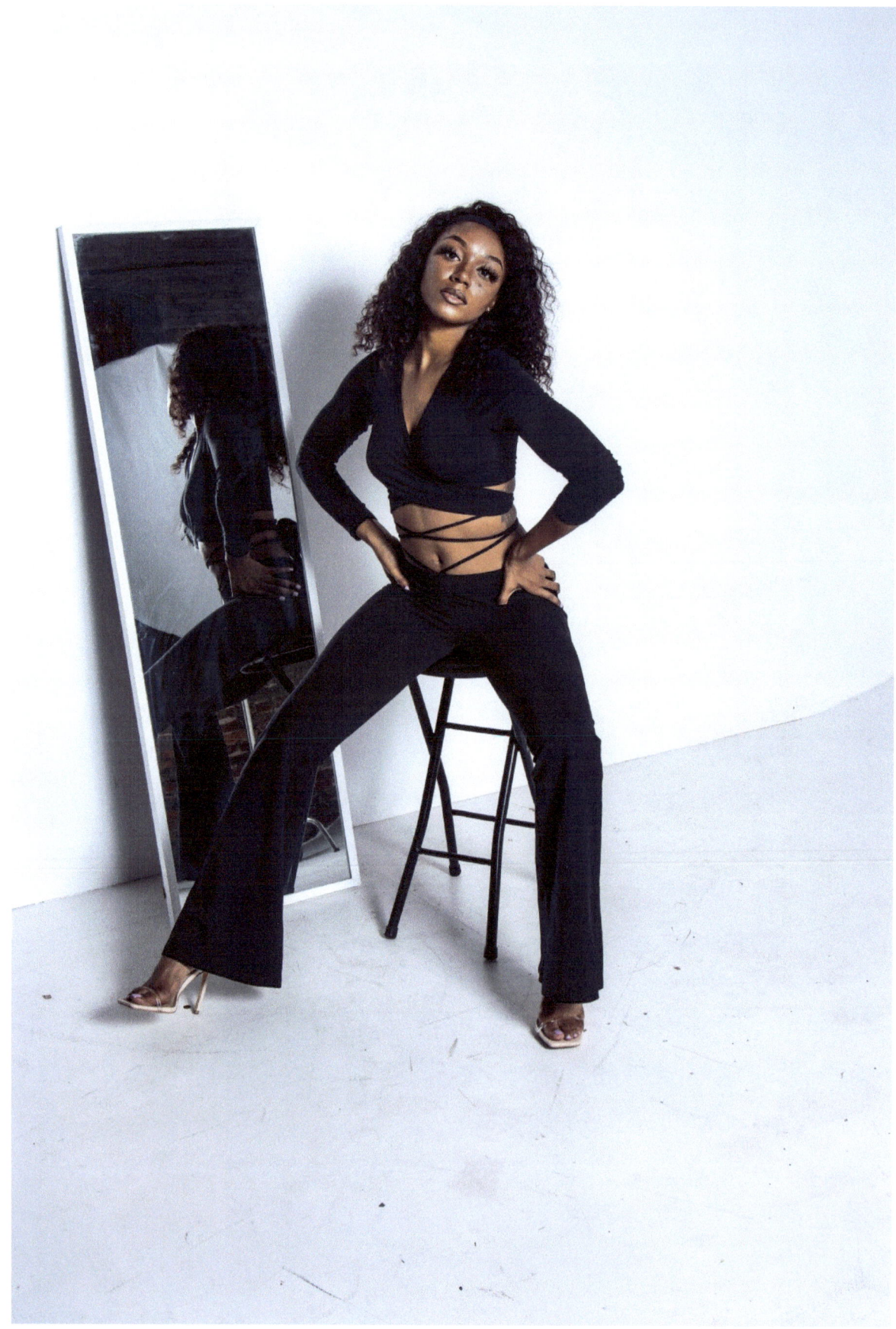

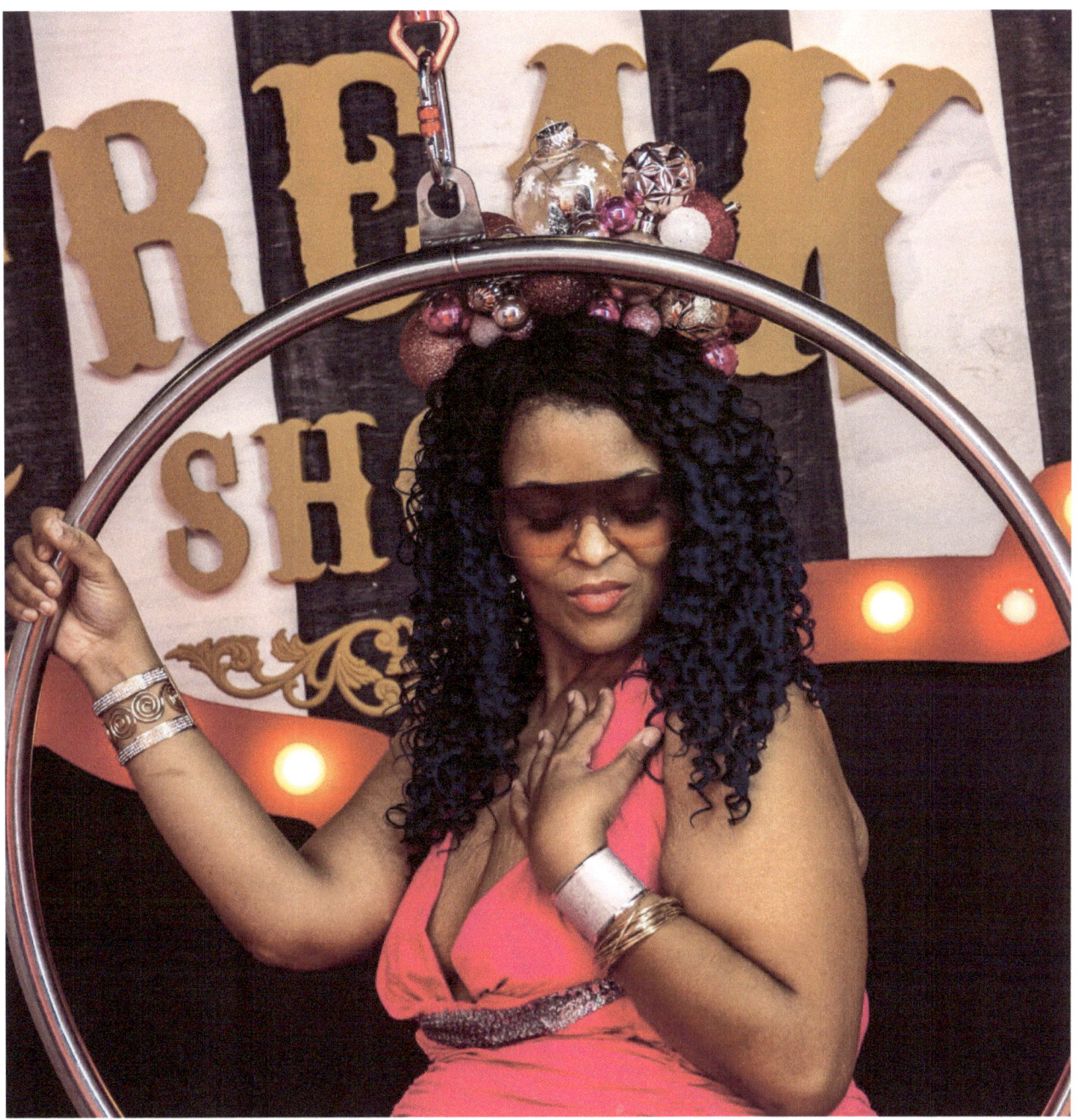

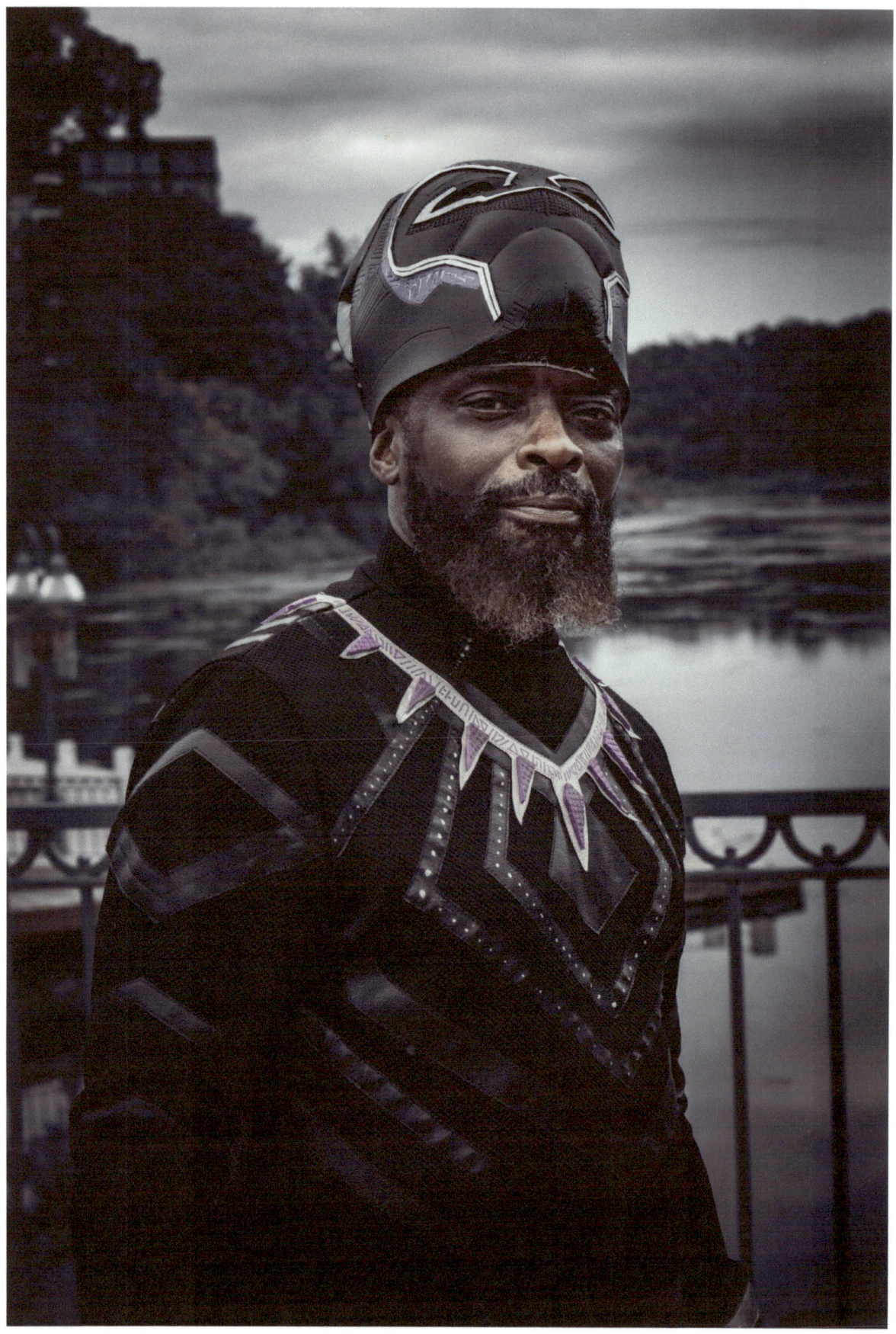

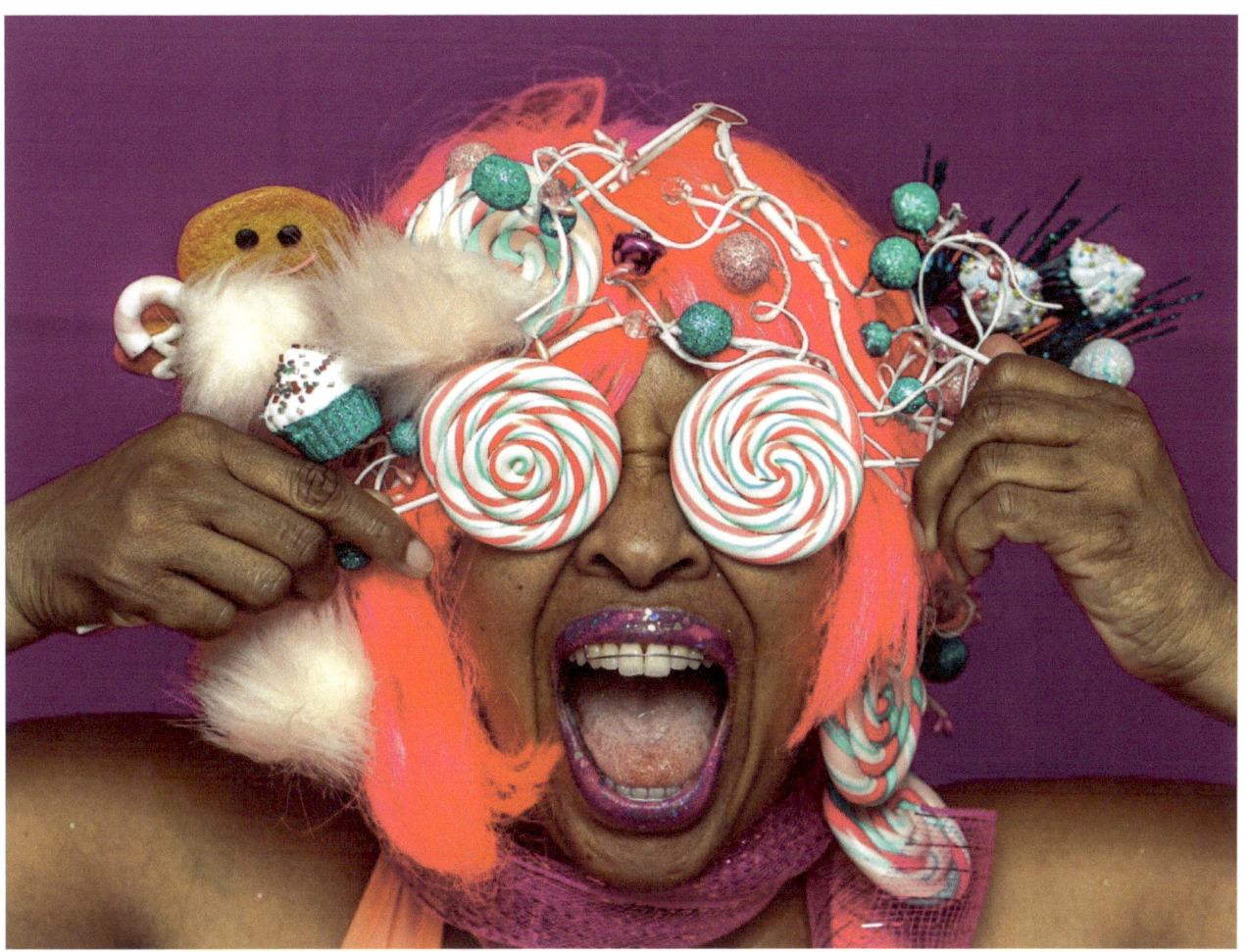

ANGIEWHITEPHOTOS.COM

Virginia Kassay

Q & A

Emmett Williams

Emmett where were you born and raised?

"I was born in Washington, D.C."

How old are you?

"I am fifty-eight years old."

Tell me about your parents. Were they the creative type?

"My mother was a Registered Nurse. When she was young, she was being trained to be a concert pianist. My father, his goal was to be an architect, but he went to war twice, so, that dream never came true. He was a Golden Gloves boxing champ in his youth. You can say he was the creative type, a "Knock-out artist." {Emmett laughs out loud)" He was the type of guy that everyone loved. Being his son was like being in the company of a famous boxer. Every time he walked down the street, he was swarmed by a bunch of kids, before he could make it to his own house. His father was an artist who became a businessperson. He owned a barber shop/beauty salon."

How many siblings if any do you have? Are they creative as well?

"There were six of us, plus mom and pop. My father died when I was seven years old. Everyone in my family is good at something. For instance, my little brother is a business wiz and my sister is a fashion designer."

What types of things interested you as a child?

"Rock 'Em Sock 'Em Robots, my slinky, magic cards and one of my favorites was Dr. Seuss Draw Along. It was cool because you finished a Dr. Seuss drawing and colored it, and the last four pages were blank. I think it said something like "Now you do something." And I never stopped."

What is your favorite memory from your childhood?

Selling comic book paintings that I created at age thirteen, for $250 a pop.

Tell me about yourself. What type of person are you?

"I am a real piece of work. Driven. Focused. I don't dream anymore. I just direct the dream while I'm in it. I influence how it comes out. I like to run the show."

Were you formally trained as an artist? Or is your talent completely raw?

"I would say that I have had formal training by studying sketches by the masters, and paintings in the library books for free. I also have paid thousands to frustrated educators in institutions, who gave up on their dreams, and taught me by default, never to do that."

Does your style reflect that of another artist or other artists, or is it uniquely your own?

'I think art is like dance. If you go back in history, not a whole lot is really that original. It's all a part of our ancestry. Also, it's marketing and that word "genius" being attributed to people and the work that makes them "seem" greater in the present.

I am a cubist, and neither I, nor Picasso, created Cubism. African artisans created the history of Cubism. They did it in 3-D sculptures and masks. Picasso studied them, and I studied Picasso. I also studied Duchamp and Braque, plus every other competent painter who had popularized the real genius of African art. In books written on Picasso, he references Cubism as "African art" more than once. I found it refreshing to see those words. Later on, it seems he was less generous about their role. Fact is, the two artists essentially starved in Paris, sacrificing funds they could have eaten with. They instead, bought up all the African sculptures and masks that they could.

I, as a painter, I appreciated the power and complexity of Cubism, having grown bored with Impressionism. I believe that Impressionism is attributable to Asian printmaking skills.

There are two modern "so-called" styles that I think have been over-looked. They are the byproducts of art created from wood. Impressionist painters mimicked the Japanese Wood-Block printing technique. African wood sculptures and masks were mimicked by Braque and Picasso."

In your opinion, what is the most interesting piece of art that you have created?

"I would say that the Chair Art Series of imagery that I created was the most interesting. I call it "PapaMamaBaba." (I own the trademark as well), I was applying sketches of it on my luggage, brief cases and jackets, when a furniture executive walked in. It was Christmas Eve. I had no heat. I created in a downtown building that I seized for myself. In a matter of minutes, I was bought out of everything that I had created, and it was all being loaded into his car. He walked back into my studio a few minutes later and wanted to sign over his Christmas bonus to commission more.

A couple of months went by. The High Point Furniture Market was quickly approaching. The guy who bought me out, had three chairs delivered to my studio. He asked that I choose three of my genres and draw them with marker on his chairs.

I could have had a reflex reaction and just did what I already knew how to do, but instead, I decided not to use the markers. I sat and thought a while until I had a new approach to offer that could not be duplicated by anyone else. I scanned the Internet for everything there was about leather. I came across a term in an artist's handbook that read " Trompe-L'oile". I applied the concept to my imagery and my imagery to the leather, to make anyone else's future claim to it seem absolutely absurd."

What inspires you to create?

"Money. Money inspires me to create. I have a desire to change the stereotypes that artists today still endure. I enjoy the exchange of art for payment. Some people dismiss artists and or try to judge us.

Here are a few examples for you regarding the importance of the role of artists in today's society.

There is enough material for a suit, a sewing machine all set up for you to use, and all you have to do is make the suit and apply for a job with said suit within twenty four hours. Will you show up naked or dressed in new suit? How important is the designer in this process?

How about this? There is a mechanic, and engineer and an assembly line ready to build you a car. How important is the designer in this process?

Or, there is enough lumber and machinery to build your dream home. Are you able to create every item needed, that goes into building a new house? Of course not, that's why there are designers and Artists. People with the vision that you need, to complete this and many other jobs out there that require a person with artistic skills.

Guess what? What if those who are skilled in creating mansions, Ferraris and haute couture fashions for you to wear, where born with weak spines and allowed others to talk them out of their destiny's? What then? Instead of soaring, what if they give up on themselves and allowed non-creative people to cannibalize all things that were the epitome of innovation, fifty years ago? Furniture and all things as we know them now and in the future, would be at a creative stand still."

When do you find, are the times, that you come up with your best ideas?

"Between 2am and 4 am."

How did the death of your beloved wife of ten years, affect you as an artist?

"Our history was one of evolution. It involved constant discussions of what was needed to get to whatever the next level was for both of our careers and in our home life. That usually involved talks about getting press coverage. But frankly, I'd been there and done that.

Our "eureka" moment was when we agreed that I ought to try and connect directly with buyers by writing about their work. My wife had read a short story that I had written for a website, and she could not stop talking about it. To me, she was the first person to point out that my style of writing could be an extension of my artwork. And then shockingly, we agreed that a graphic novel would be the direction to head in. There is more to selling art than painting a picture. That was the ultimate realization for me. And depending on even a "willing" press, is still dependence.

After my wife passed, I worked on my magazine. I self-branded it like I wanted the logo to be remembered for the next 500 years. I used it to distract me from the painful five-year long memories that flooded my brain. I had to deal with the legal drama with the family I was married into. It was overwhelming. I was told that I had no chance of winning a case I had against her family, from three lawyers, one of which was mine. I am the type of person who has always been told what I can't do, by so-called "wise" people, yet I have always won anyway. As a child I focused on King David. I saw each and every obstacle as Goliath, big and threatening. So as long as I knew that I was David in the scenario, I knew my obstacles were as good as conquered on arrival.

When did you come up with the idea for EM?

"I actually came up with the idea for doing a magazine about fifteen years ago, but I allowed myself to be talked out of naming it after me. I'd been creating comics since I was around eight years old. Older and wiser now, I realized that maybe other people would be interested in the same artists that I was interested in. I just needed to change my Cubist experience of assembling images, my comic book skills and writing skills, into a magazine format. Instead of creating interesting characters, I found real characters that are interesting. Then I could introduce the artwork of my friends and colleagues to the world as well."

You have no formal training in the magazine publishing industry. Do see EM becoming a great success despite your limited knowledge?

"I decided that whatever every other publication out there was doing, it was leading them into the abyss.

Whatever their beginnings, whatever got their publications off the ground, were now dead and buried. In order to achieve anything, you have to have a vision or be a visionary to lead it to success. I just decided to stop listening to people and stop asking permission to do great things. I don't know the formalities of creating a magazine, according to past standards. Most of the newspapers and magazines I grew up with are no longer in publication. I will run my magazine the way I run everything in my life. I wake up every day and before I repeat the day before, I wonder to myself, if there is a better more efficient way to get what I need to get done. Is there a smarter, cheaper, faster way. I see it as the more wasted time I recover in a day, the more I can refocus on being more effective.

I ask myself these questions:

Who has the skills, I need to add to it?

Who do I really want to know about?

What can I offer them to get what I want?

What is going on in the world that is worth talking about?

Whose artwork, if not my own, would I want to see on the pages of my magazine?

Do I need to go outside of my comfort zone and seek people outside the U.S. to write for me?

I know "So and So" paints, do they have any other skills that can contribute to my magazine?

Do you create anything besides canvas art? I know we touched on the furniture industry a little while back in the interview. Maybe you can elaborate.

I hand-painted leather furniture, instead of using markers like I had originally used in the beginning. I started around 2003 with North Carolina furniture companies. Now I design my own furniture prototypes and am in the process of creating the pieces I designed. I need to find people who can sew leather and build my designs better than I can. I also enjoy welding steel sculptures, but I find myself unable to part with them. I sold all but one that I just can't let go of. I like working with wire. I also like working with ceramics, but the piece I created that I loved the most, broke into pieces in my hands. I think I need to go to fiberglass. I love making plastic sculptures. I just want to make them on a giant scale."

Who are your favorite artists? And why?

"Painters would be Marcel Duchamp, Frida Kahlo, Salvador Dali, Pablo Picasso, Jacob Lawrence and Tamara de Lempicka.

If I had to name my top two, they would be Duchamp and Lempicka. When was around eleven or twelve, I was refused participation in a life drawing class. So instead, I started studying books by the masters from the library. Once I saw what was in the books, I had no intention of giving them back. I became obsessed with the descending the staircase by Duchamp. I though it was incredibly interesting, as it a power of me, and conveyed complex movement in one frame. I had seen a ton of Picasso's works and although they were powerful and compelling, they did not have the sublime grace that this one painting by Duchamp did. So something called "Library Amnesty" was created. Seemingly just for me. I returned the Picasso books, and paid for the Duchamp books that I refused to return."

"How I see these artists works":

"Dali- Unpredictable and visually compelling

Picasso- Powerful

Jacob Lawrence- Not a cartoonist, but he has excellent story-telling techniques, powerful and unique.

Kahlo- She turns tragedy into treasure. She depicts her own unconquerable will and spirit in her works.

DeLempicka- Power and beauty."

"I worked in a museum which exhibited DeLempicka. I felt more comfortable turning my drawings into beautiful cubist woman after viewing what they called "Deco". It was Cubism, pure and simple, but for some reason, it seemed that the art world wanted to reserve the term "Cubism", for Picasso alone. So they gave her work a prettier, more feminine adjective, which in my opinion is ridiculous. I've heard it said that she "painted like a man." No. She was a Cubist, so she painted like a Cubist and the models were both beautiful and powerful at the same time. Seeing her works in person, seemed to almost give me permission to do whatever the bleep I needed to do, to have my imagery pop off the walls."

"Cartoonists/Illustrators":

Jack Kirby, John Romita, Steve Ditko, Alex Ross and Charles Schulz.

I chose these people for their talent and their decency. I saw their works regarding African Americans and they are respectful. Also, in a time when no one else dared to depict other races with respect, they did and or still do."

" If I was on an deserted island and had to choose one, it would be Jack Kirby. In my opinion, still seeing his output from fifty years ago or more, he is ten times better than most of the best comic book creators there have ever been and ever will be. Inked or not. If I could wake up and be able to tell my untold stories as efficiently as Kirby, I would care less about comparisons and just do it. The process is o time consuming that you just must have a visionary team on the same page (metaphor) what worked for Disney in animation worked for Marvel, the House-Style concept is not only a time-saver it is necessary, and excellent training for anyone studying the Master, Jack Kirby. The entire genre of "Pop Art" was *inspired* (nice word), by his imagery."

How often do you create?

"I create in numerous forms these days. Fifty percent writing, twenty-five percent layout/cover design and the rest is art/laborious inking, of stories still trying to get told properly. I am not the best inker, so I try to keep it simple but interesting in order to move the story along."

Do you feel the need to create on a daily basis? What happens if you can't?

"That never happens. If I'm out of town, I would compel someone to give me some paper and a pen. I do something creative every day. I can go for months without the urge to create a painting, but I draw twenty to thirty images every single day."

Please tell me some of the places that you have exhibited.

"WFMY news2 on "The Good Morning Show Gallery" which featured my piece called "The Blues guitarist." Web traffic crashed my site and it sold by the end of the day. I was also a guest on the show."

"The Greenville Museum of Art in North Carolina in an exhibition. Cubist Woman. The Bass Player, Modern Mona and Still Life No. 7 were the pieces that I exhibited. It was a group exhibition called "Living Artists of North Carolina." I got to show with my friend Floyd Newkirk and other North Carolina notables."

"The Phoenix Home and Garden Magazine Expo". My original artwork and hand-painted furniture sold out twice as the company re-ordered the sold furniture and then sold that."

And at "The Bellagio Hotel and Casino", were four hand-painted chairs commissioned by a New York designer with my art on them that were exhibited.

Which of your exhibits was your favorite, and why?

"STREETFACE" an urban experience, in 2019. It was a solo exhibition, my last exhibit for a couple of reasons. My wife was in it with me for one. She was a lawyer by trade, but she taught herself how to make molds and casted items, excelling in her craft even through her cancers. I don't humor anyone when it comes to joint exhibitions, where I have the final say, but she was worthy. I was one of her only subjects, and she made some casts of my face. With those casts, we then collaborated on a 3-D piece for the "STREETFACE" exhibit, which was the theme of the show. A few of her colleagues from her job came through, and we also created our own playlists, over several months. There was fantastic live Blues music and food there as well. The exhibition turned out to be spectacular. I was invited to exhibit twice there before the "STREETFACE" exhibition."

Where do you see yourself in the future?

" I'm already here. I know I'm doing exactly what I am supposed to be doing, right now." Life experience tells me, when things fall into place as quickly as they are now, it means that I am in the right place mentally and physically."

How can someone purchase one of your pieces?

"You can E-mail me directly at Publisher@EmmettMagazine.com.

Ask for pricing if it's an existing work, you've seen and are interested in purchasing. Or you can commission something in your price range, even if it's a thumbnail sketch for a few dollars."

2022

Here We Come!

www.ingramcontent.com/pod-product-compliance
Lightning Source LLC
Chambersburg PA
CBHW040412220526
45473CB00004B/1214

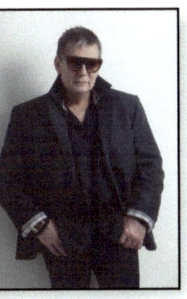

HJR Balaguer
Publisher

New York City - Collection Spring / Summer 2022

IN SEARCH OF BEAUTY

Trend inspiration

From New York to Milan from London to Paris and then from Barcelona to LA, urban color has become the star of the international artistic hair and music events, winning hair-trends are always transformable, never predictable. Hair, make-up and fashion are the living frescos of the modern-day look, a dreaming fairy-tale for a woman that is a romantic heroine, shapes and forms as highlight femininity where luxury is queen. A healthy desire to take the limelight again or to be protagonist now and then, hi-technology in in your definition, giving a newer face to your urban-tunes that "sets-off" your under-dimensional groove exalting your own projection in hair fashion lines becomes the blazing star of Twenty-Twenty-Two 2022 Hair Fashion Collection.

Creation

Vintage elements inspire a modern urban look as the extraordinary magic from intense glazes, reminiscent of the new industrial era, metallic effects in dark-light atmospheres. Discreetly elegant choices that seduces at first sight like a painter, a palette of colors knows no-limit, sandy blonde reflections are immersed in coral, silver and gold hues Supported by precision in design as style discovers simplicity. In total nakedness of women or men reveal themselves with only a few special objects that exalting your musical trend with screaming violent audacity. Following-up of this exalted concoction of jam-packed with whole-hog-hand spirited flow RnB & Trap into new depths of RnB mixed Trap to enhance your own hit-oriented commercial productions. Carry-on! To surpass ourselves is to arrive at the excellence of your work with a complete program in music formation; from technical learning or specialization to enterprise management, marketing and sales.

Celebration

Ancient values are re-embraced as a nomadic soul facing new horizons in love with open spaces music flows in-harmony as it follows the ebb flowing thru the breeze. Your freedom in thoughts; freedom in movement from electric blue or petroleum green made in high-precision engraved with thousand strands of light. Broken-lines of alternative undercuts follows around perimeters, and the it's turn for blondes and reds, refined elegance brimming with nuances in the desert, maybe a seduction of an intellectual dreamer into a free spirit for music's longing intimacy. To prevail together; all-together is the objective of our activities with an animation of continuous development in business with mass-media and diffusion and musical image, oh well, soon you'll know what I mean jelly-bean.

Trend inspiration

Desde Nueva York a Milán, desde Londres a París y luego desde Barcelona a Los Ángeles, el color urbano se ha convertido en la estrella de los eventos artísticos internacionales de cabello y música, las tendencias ganadoras de cabello siempre son transformables, nunca predecibles. El cabello, el maquillaje y la moda son los frescos vivos del look moderno, un cuento de hadas de ensueño para una mujer que es una heroína, romántica y las formas que resaltan la feminidad donde el lujo es la reina. Un deseo saludable de volver a ser el centro de atención o ser protagonista de vez en cuando, la alta tecnología en su definición, dando una nueva cara a sus melodías urbanas que "desencadenan" su surco sub-dimensional exaltando su propia proyección en el cabello. Las líneas de moda se convierten en la estrella ardiente de Twenty-Twenty-Two 2022 Collectiones de Moda Cabello.

Creation

Los elementos vintage inspiran un aspecto urbano moderno como la extraordinaria magia de los esmaltes intensos, que recuerdan la nueva era industrial, los efectos metálicos en ambientes de luz oscura. Elecciones discretamente elegantes que seducen a primera vista como un pintor, una paleta de colores que conoce sin límites, los reflejos rubios arenosos están inmersos en tonos coral, plateado y dorado Apoyados por la precisión en el diseño a medida que el estilo descubre la sencillez, en la desnudez total de mujeres u hombres, se revelan con solo unos pocos objetos especiales que exaltan su tendencia musical con audacia violenta. El seguimiento de esta mezcla exaltada de RnB & Trap repleto de RnB & Trap lleno de mano de cerdo en las nuevas profundidades de RnB Mixed Trap para mejorar sus propias producciones comerciales orientadas al éxito. ¡Continua! Superarnos a nosotros mismos es llegar a la excelencia de su trabajo con un programa completo en formación musical; desde aprendizaje técnico o especialización hasta gestión empresarial, marketing y ventas.

Celebration

Los valores antiguos se vuelven a abrazar como un alma nómada que enfrenta nuevos horizontes enamorados de los espacios abiertos, la música fluye en armonía mientras sigue el flujo que fluye a través de la brisa. Tu libertad en los pensamientos; libertad de movimiento desde el azul eléctrico o el verde petrolero realizado en alta precisión grabado con miles de hilos de luz. Siguen líneas discontinuas de socavaciones alternativas alrededor de los perímetros, y es el momento de las rubias y los rojos, la elegancia refinada rebosante de matices en el desierto, tal vez la seducción de un soñador intelectual en un espíritu libre para la intimidad anhelante de la música. Para prevalecer juntos; Todo junto es el objetivo de nuestras actividades con una animación de desarrollo continuo en los negocios con medios de comunicación y difusión e imagen musical, bueno, pronto sabrán a qué me refiero con gominolas.

**Hairworld International and you. An unique association.
To dream, to surpass ourselves, to prevail... together..**

Hairworld International

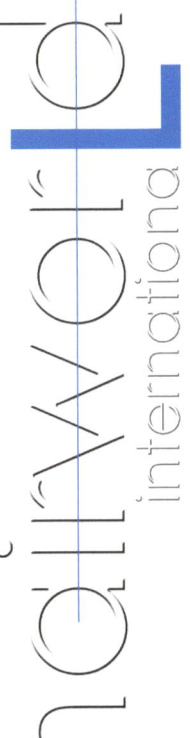

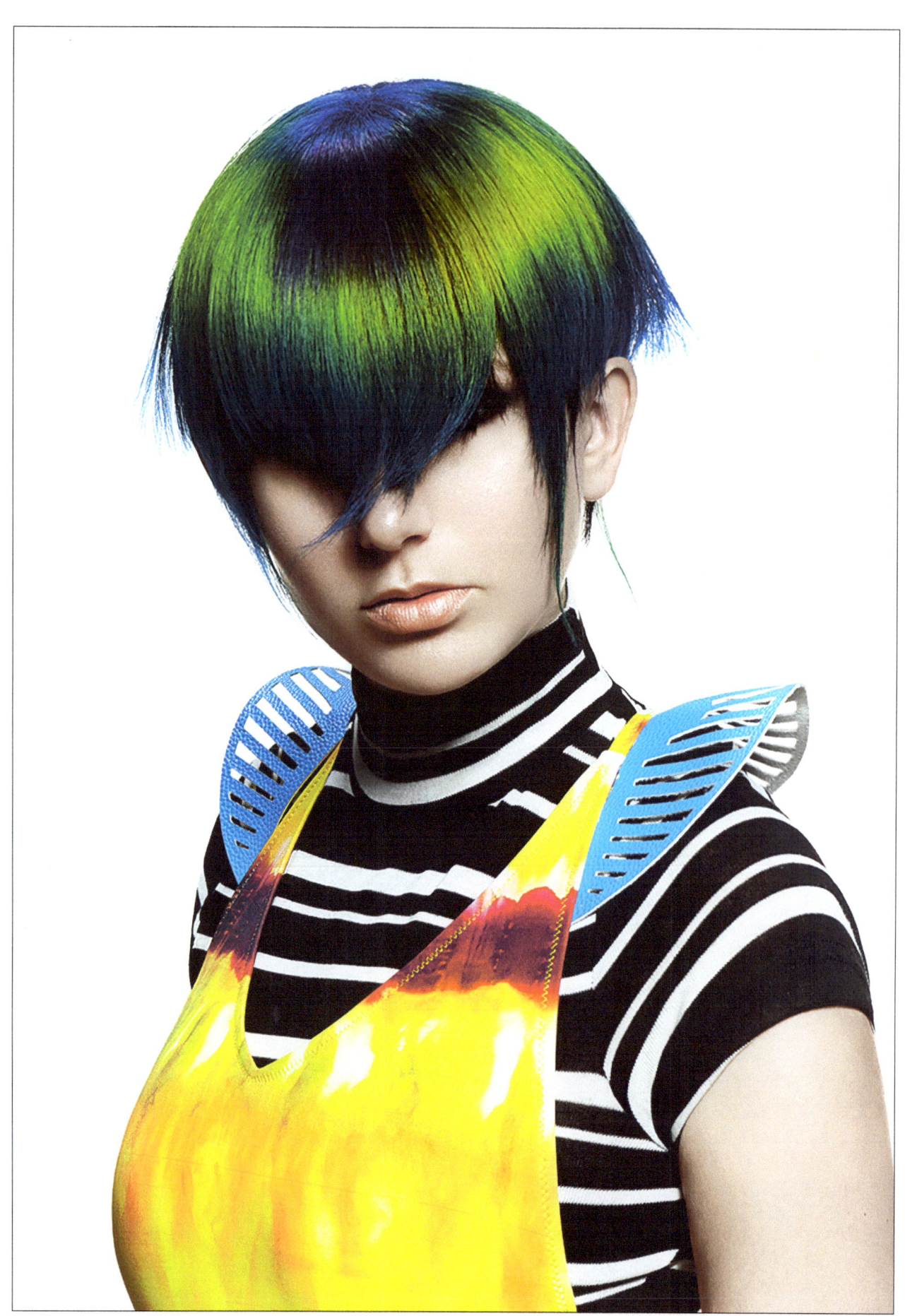

Hair: Chrystofer Benson Team - Make-up: Danielle Donahue - Photography: John Rawson